UNDERSTANDING THE CATECHISM
Morality

D0406580

MICHAEL PENNOCK

RESOURCES FOR CHRISTIAN LIVING™
Allen, Texas

> "The Ad Hoc Committee to Oversee
> the Use of the Catechism,
> National Conference of Catholic Bishops,
> has found this catechetical text
> to be in conformity with
> the *Catechism of the Catholic Church*."

NIHIL OBSTAT
Rev. Msgr. Glenn D. Gardner, J.C.D.
Censor Librorum

IMPRIMATUR
† Most Rev. Charles V. Grahmann
Bishop of Dallas

April 27, 1998

The Nihil Obstat and Imprimatur are official declarations that the material reviewed is free of doctrinal or moral error. No implication is contained therein that those granting the Nihil Obstat and Imprimatur agree with the contents, opinions, or statements expressed.

Send all inquiries to:
RCL • Resources for Christian Living®
200 East Bethany Drive
Allen, Texas 75002-3804

Toll Free   877-275-4725
Fax   800-688-8356

Visit us at www.rclweb. com
Visit us at www.faithfirst.com

Printed in the United States of America

20254   ISBN 0-7829-0876-4 (Student Book)
20255   ISBN 0-7829-0877-2 (Teacher's Guide)

6 7 8 9 10 11 12

05 06 07 08 09 10

ACKNOWLEDGMENTS

Scripture selections are taken from the *New American Bible* © 1991, 1986, 1970 by the Confraternity of Christian Doctrine, Washington, D.C. and are used by license of the copyright owner. All rights reserved. No part of the New American Bible may be used or reproduced in any form, without the permission of the copyright owner.

Excerpts from the English translation of the *Catechism of the Catholic Church* for the United States of America copyright © 1994 United States Catholic Conference, Inc.—Libreria Editrice Vaticana. Used with permission.

Excerpts from *Vatican Council II: The Conciliar and Post Conciliar Documents, New Revised Edition*, Austin Flannery, O.P., Gen. Ed. Copyright © 1975, 1986, 1992, 1996 by Costello Publishing Company, Inc. Used by permission.

Excerpt from *The Splendor of Truth*. Pope John Paul II, Copyright © 1994 by St. Paul Books and Media. Used by permission.

Excerpts from CD ROM: *Catholic Desktop Library*. Copyright © 1994–1995, by Pauline Books and Media. Used by permission.

Excerpts from *The Vatican Council II: Volume 1, The Conciliar and Postconciliar Documents*. Austin Flannery. O.P., Gen. Ed. Copyright © 1975, by Costello Publishing Company, Inc. Used by permission.

Excerpt from *On the Family*. Pope John Paul II, Copyright © 1982, by United States Catholic Conference, Inc. Used by permission.

Excerpts from *The Gospel of Life*. Pope John Paul II, by United States Catholic Conference, Inc. Used by permission.

Excerpt from *Pastoral Letters of the United States Catholic Bishops*. Hugh J. Nolan, Editor. Copyright © 1984, by United States Catholic Conference, Inc. Used by permission.

Excerpt from *Catholic Household Blessings and Prayers*. Copyright © 1989, by United States Catholic Conference, Inc. Used by permission.

Excerpts from *The Rites of the Catholic Church*. Copyright © 1976, by Pueblo Publishing Company, Inc. Used by permission.

Excerpt from *Compton's Reference Collection 1996*. Copyright © 1995, by Compton's NewMedia, Inc. Used by permission.

Excerpts from *The Wisdom of the Saints: An Anthology*. Jill Haak Adels, Editor. Copyright © 1987, by Oxford University Press, Inc. Used by permission.

Excerpts from *Letting God: Christian Meditations for Recovering Persons*. A Philip Parham. Copyright © 1987, by HarperCollins Publishers. Used by permission.

Excerpts from *Father McBride's Teen Catechism*. Alfred McBride, O. Praem. Copyright © 1995, by Good Will Publishers, Inc. Used by permission.

Excerpt from *God's Little Devotional Book for Men*. W.B. Freeman Concepts. Ed. Copyright © 1996, by Honor Books, Inc. Used by permission.

Excerpt from *Praise Him: A Prayerbook for Today's Christian*. Copyright © 1973, by Ave Maria Press. Used by permission.

Excerpt from *The Spiritual Exercises of Saint Ignatious*. George E. Ganss, S. J., Translator. Copyright 1992, by Loyola University Press. Used by permission.

Photos: © Scott Barrow/International Stock, 70; Catholic News Service, 43; Corbis-Bettmann, 15; © Bob Firth/International Stock, 114; Full Photographics, 68; Jeff Greenberg/Unicorn Stock Photos, 76; © Michael Krasowitz/FPG International, 109; Major League Baseball Properties, 32; Powerstock Photo/Index Stock Photography, 58; SW Production/Index Stock Photography, 80; Scott Thode/International Stock, 84; Jim Sulley, The ImageWorks, 106; © Bill Wittman, 20, 23, 46; Donald F. Wristen, 135.

Contents

Introduction

Welcome to this book on principles and foundations of Catholic morality. It derives its inspiration from the *Catechism of the Catholic Church* (CCC), which was published in October 1992. The Catechism presents the essential teachings of our Catholic faith authoritatively, systematically, and comprehensively.

The source of the teachings of our Catholic faith is Sacred Scripture and Sacred Tradition, both of which pass on to us divine Revelation. Our official church teachers, which we call the Magisterium of the Church, authentically interpret and pass this revelation on to us.

The Catechism is a remarkable resource book for all Catholics. It is divided into four main parts. The four parts have come to be called the four pillars, or foundations, of the Catechism. They are:

❑ The Profession of Faith (The Creed)
❑ The Celebration of the Christian Mystery (Worship: Liturgy and Sacraments)
❑ Life in Christ (Moral Living)
❑ Christian Prayer

The Catechism is more than seven hundred pages in its English translation. As a result, the Catechism itself encourages us to adapt it. This book, *Understanding the Catechism: Morality,* is one part of a four-book series on the Catechism. This series has been especially written for Catholic high school students.

Understanding the Catechism: Morality will introduce you to the major content of the third part of the Catechism—Life in Christ. It will introduce you to or review for you the moral teachings of the Church that guide us in living our life in Christ.

"The first is this: 'Hear, O Israel! The Lord our God is Lord alone! You shall love the Lord your God with all your heart, with all your soul, with all your mind, and with all your strength.' The second is this: 'You shall love your neighbor as yourself.' "

Mark 12:29–31

CHAPTER 1

Basics of Catholic Morality: Be Who You Are!

"If you remain in my word,
you will truly be my disciples,
and you will know the truth,
and the truth will set you free."
JOHN 8:31–32

KEY TERMS

Beatitudes

freedom

free will

morality

Who are the happiest people on earth? A newspaper from Britain once asked this question of its readers. The four prize-winning answers were:

❏ A small child having fun building sand castles.

❏ An artist standing back and admiring her beautiful creation.

❏ An exhausted doctor who has just completed a difficult operation that saved a human life.

❏ A mother who bathes and then cuddles her baby at the end of a busy day.

What do these people have in common? They throw themselves into life and do something that gives them a sense of accomplishment and meaning. Someone once observed that there are three ingredients to happiness: something to do, something to love, something to hope for. All these people seem to meet these criteria.

Who are the happiest people you know? What is the secret to their happiness? How do you define _happiness?_

[7]

Happiness is a by-product of living a Christian life. Jesus Christ came to make us happy and to show us the way to our eternal destiny, where we will obtain that total happiness which we all crave. The secret to happiness is simply this: Live a life of love. Imitate God our Father by putting on the mind of Jesus Christ, conforming our thoughts, words, and actions to him. Drawing on the teaching of the *Catechism of the Catholic Church,* this text, *Understanding the Catechism: Morality,* will explain how to live a moral life in Christ.

(Catechism of the Catholic Church, 1701–1709, 1730–1742)

Christian Moral Living

Christian morality is responsible Christian living. Its essence is love. Jesus summarized the way we are to live when he taught:

> "You shall love the Lord, your God, with all your heart, with all your soul, and with all your mind. This is the greatest and the first commandment. The second is like it: You shall love your neighbor as yourself."
>
> Matthew 22:37–39

Christian moral living involves an ability to respond to God's own gift of love and salvation in Christ Jesus. Without ever destroying our freedom, the Holy Spirit empowers us to say yes to Jesus and to live in conformity to God's plan for us. Christian moral living requires our free response to God's invitation to live as a child of God. We must actively strive to live three key principles:

❏ Be the human person God calls us to be.

❏ Do good and avoid evil.

❏ Be a Beatitude person.

A Christian View of the Human Person

If we strive to live a Christlike, loving life, we will be who we really are: children of God, created in the image and likeness of God and invited to share in the joy and life of God. Living such a life is our way to discover and enjoy happiness.

We are made in God's image and likeness. Christians hold a tremendously optimistic picture of humans. In fact, we believe humans are fundamentally good because God created us in his image and likeness, conforming us to Jesus Christ who is "the image of the invisible God."

Being made in the divine image, we possess a spiritual and immortal soul that has the ability to think (an intellect) and the power to choose and to love (free will). We humans are unique among earth's creatures because God made us for himself, giving us a destiny of eternal happiness (or "beatitude").

Because we image God and are God's special creatures, each human being has incomparable worth from the first moment of conception. Each of us has tremendous dignity and value that do not have to be earned. We possess the ability to live a Christian moral life.

What the Documents Say

Freedom is the power, rooted in reason and will, to act or not to act, to do this or that, and so to perform deliberate actions on one's own responsibility. By free will one shapes one's own life. Human freedom is a force for growth and maturity in truth and goodness; it attains its perfection when directed toward God, our beatitude.

(CCC, 1731)

Discuss: Human freedom is a force for growth and maturity. What are some of the difficulties you face in exercising your freedom?

We can think. Our intellects enable us to recognize God's voice in our conscience. We can understand God's command to do good and avoid evil, to identify what is loving and what is not. When we follow through on what we know is right, we are living a moral life and allowing our dignity to shine through.

We can choose. Free will enables us to desire and then choose what is good. When we choose the good of others, we love. Loving and choosing to do what is true and good fulfills us as humans.

We are free. The capacities to reason and to choose reflect God's image. Together they give freedom to us. True **freedom** empowers us to act or not to act, to perform actions for which we are personally responsible. We exercise our freedom in relationship to others whom we must respect as made in God's image, who are also free and responsible like us. All humans have an inalienable right to exercise their freedom, especially in moral and religious matters. Within the limits of the common good and social order, governments have a duty to recognize and protect this fundamental right essential to human dignity.

When we exercise our freedom in accord with God's Law, we are doing good, acting morally, and becoming truly free. On the other hand, when we refuse to keep God's Law, we do evil, abuse our freedom, and become slaves to sin.

We are wounded by sin. Salvation history tells the story of how our first parents abused their freedom by disobeying God and giving in to the Evil One. Their original sin wounded human nature. Though we still desire what is good, we are divided within ourselves, inclined to do evil and prone to making mistakes. Within us as individuals and as a race rages a battle between good and evil, light and darkness. Our freedom is limited and subject to error.

We are children of God. Yet, there is good news! Christ's passion, death, and resurrection have delivered us from sin and the Evil One. Christ has gained for us a new life in the Holy Spirit. Through God's grace and the gifts of faith and baptism, God adopts us into the divine family. We become children of God. The Spirit of Christ lives in us to help us make moral choices, do good, and love as he loves. Cooperating with Christ's grace increases our inner, spiritual freedom that helps us to do good and to live according to God's plan.

We are friends of the Lord! In fact, not only do we Christians have good news about our identity—we have great news! In a remarkable passage in John's Gospel, Jesus tells us that we are his friends. (See John 15:11–17.)

Note several features of this marvelous passage. First, Jesus tells us about the reality of his friendship so we might be joyful. The truth about his relationship to us does indeed bring us joy. How could we not be happy having the Savior of the world, who sacrificed his life for us, call *us*—mere creatures—*his* friends? What inestimable worth he sees in us. How valuable we are in his eyes. Other friends may let us down, but the Lord Jesus never will.

Second, Jesus does not relate to us as servants who are ignorant about what is happening. No, Jesus relates to us as friends and reveals to us all that his Father told him. He singles each of us out and befriends us. By choosing us he has taken the initiative in the friendship relationship. And he invites us to approach his Father, trusting in his paternal love and mercy. We need never fear with Jesus as our friend and Savior and his Father as our Abba, our loving Father whom we trust unconditionally, who looks out for our every need.

Third, Jesus asks one thing in return— that we love one another. This is the very heart of Christian morality.

What does it mean to be responsible for our actions? (CCC, 1731–1742)

The freedom to choose between good and evil is what characterizes human acts. When freedom is not bound to God totally as the greatest good, it is possible for humans to choose between good and evil. If we choose good, we grow in love. If we knowingly and freely choose evil, we sin.

Certain factors can lessen or destroy blameworthiness for our actions. Examples include ignorance that is not our fault, inattention, fear, force, and habit.

Freedom is not a license to say or do whatever we want. Human history is filled with the sad results of misused or misdirected freedom. Because of original sin, we sometimes choose an earthly good like power, prestige, money, or sex and turn it into a god. Societal, political, and economic factors can also threaten true human freedom, tempting us as individuals and groups to live selfishly and unlovingly. To choose contrary to God's will makes us slaves to sin.

Brainstorm ways you see human freedom being abused in society. What results from that abuse?

Accepting Jesus' friendship, we show our love for him and his loving Father by loving each other. If we do live lovingly, we will truly have a joy-filled, happy life.

For Christians, living a moral life means living according to the teachings of Jesus. Obeying his teachings brings life and joy. Read and reflect on these gospel passages. In the space provided, briefly summarize what Jesus is teaching us, his followers.

1. **Mark 9:33–37**

2. **Luke 6:36–38**

3. **John 15:11–17**

4. **Matthew 19:16–30**

•••• Discuss

Which of the above teachings makes the most sense? Which is the toughest to put into practice? Which is most needed in today's world?

Considering the above points, we can conclude that we act morally when we responsibly use our God-given intellects and wills, when we choose good and avoid evil, and when we act as persons of incomparable worth who respect the essential dignity of others. We act morally when we cooperate with the Holy Spirit who lives in us. We act morally when we are Christlike, responding as a son or daughter of a loving Father. We are moral when we act as a true friend of Jesus would, showing our love for God by loving our neighbor.

(CCC, 1716–1724)

God Created Us for Happiness

Why did God create you?" Without a doubt, this is one of the really important questions in life. Christianity teaches: Out of his great love, God created us to be happy. It is that simple, yet that profound.

God made us to know, love, and serve him in this life and to be happy with him forever in the afterlife. God made us for happiness, for "beatitude." He implanted in us a tremendous, insatiable thirst for happiness that only he can satisfy. God made us to share in his divine nature, to partake of the vision of God.

The happiness, or beatitude, God desires for us is his total gift to us. However, we must learn how to accept this gift. In short, our part of the equation is to make good moral choices throughout our life so we may obtain true happiness. Part of our learning process is understanding that fame, fortune, power, pleasure, or any other human achievement in and of itself

cannot and will never bring us true happiness. The true source of our happiness is putting God first in our lives—above all created things—and doing God's will.

We must continually purify our hearts and rid ourselves of our bad habits so that we can fully seek and embrace God's love. We will only find true happiness by living responsible, moral lives indicated by the Ten Commandments, Jesus' Sermon on the Mount, and the instruction of the apostles and the **Magisterium** of the Church.

Special Role of the Beatitudes

We find the heart of Jesus' preaching in the Beatitudes. Listed at the beginning of the famous Sermon on the Mount, they summarize Christian and New Testament morality. The Beatitudes have a privileged role in Christian moral teaching because they fulfill the promises Yahweh made to Abraham. They teach us the path to true happiness that God implanted in our hearts, the kingdom of Heaven.

The Beatitudes teach us proper Christian attitudes and actions, showing us how to act as the daughters and sons of the loving Triune God who invites us to share his life. With God's grace, they teach us how to attain our eternal destiny and give us hope in the midst of suffering. They also tell us about the rewards Christ has already won for his true disciples.

The Beatitudes are so important that all Christians should know them by heart. Moreover, we should continuously strive to put them into practice so they become part of our "attitudes of being" a follower of Jesus Christ.

The Beatitudes and Your Christian Journey

How well are you currently living the Beatitudes of Jesus? How would you evaluate yourself on following Christ's blueprint of attitudes and actions for being his disciple? For each beatitude, evaluate yourself, using this key: 1 means you are very positive and strong in living this beatitude; on the other hand, 5 means you have a long, long way to go. Follow these instructions:

❑ Read the explanation of the beatitude given.

❑ Reflect on the questions asked.

❑ Rate yourself appropriately—and honestly.

**"Blessed are the poor in spirit,
    for theirs is the kingdom of heaven"** (Matthew 5:3).

We are poor in spirit when we recognize that everything we are and everything we have (intelligence, health, talents, possessions, and so on) are pure gifts from God. We are generous and show our thanks to God by sharing with others.

Reflect: Do you admit your need for God? Do you thank him for your gifts? Do you share the gift of yourself—talent, time, possessions, and so on—with others?

1   2   3   4   5

**"Blessed are they who mourn,
    for they will be comforted"** (Matthew 5:4).

We mourn when we are sorrowful over a sinful world and over our own sins. We are saddened over injustice—children who are homeless and hungry; people denied basic human rights like the right to life, economic opportunity; people whose lives are tragically shattered because of drug abuse, misused sexuality, prejudice, war, and so on. Such lamenting can lead us to action to help correct the many problems that keep people from God.

Reflect: Do you feel the pain of friends and others who are being victimized? Do you lament the evil influences in society and try to resist their subtle allures? Do you regret your own sins and failures to love God?

1   2   3   4   5

**"Blessed are the meek,
   for they will inherit the land"** (Matthew 5:5).

We are meek when we accept others with compassion and gentility. We suffer quietly when hurt and are despised. We imitate Jesus when we suffer the human weaknesses others inflict on us and work with gentle persistence to solve problems without hatred, violence, or ill will.

Reflect: Are you a gentle person, patient with yourself and others? Are you humble and unassuming? Do you lift others up without inflating your own ego?

1   2   3   4   5

**"Blessed are they who hunger and thirst for righteousness,
   for they will be satisfied"** (Matthew 5:6).

We hunger and thirst for righteousness when we desire and work for God's will and seek God's ways above all else. We seek to grow in uprightness and holiness.

Reflect: Can you truly say that you are making your relationship with Jesus your top priority? When you pray the Lord's Prayer, do you really mean "Thy will be done"?

1   2   3   4   5

**"Blessed are the merciful,
   for they will be shown mercy"** (Matthew 5:7).

We are merciful when we image God's merciful love to others—and to ourselves. We forgive others, especially our enemies. We let Christ's compassion shine through with our words and actions. Jesus died on the cross forgiving his enemies. In the Lord's Prayer, he teaches us to forgive others.

Reflect: Do you forgive those who have hurt you? Can you let others forgive you? Can you sense the hurting person and reach out in love to him or her?

1   2   3   4   5

**"Blessed are the clean of heart,
   for they will see God"** (Matthew 5:8).

We are clean [pure] of heart when we are undivided in our loyalties toward God. We are committed to God as our top priority. Money, job, family, friends, play, school, popularity, and everything else fall in place behind our relationship to God.

Reflect: How loyal are you in your commitment to God? Do you know what your priorities are?

1   2   3   4   5

**"Blessed are the peacemakers,
  for they will be called children of God"** (Matthew 5:9).

We are peacemakers when we do not cause or seek violence and conflict. We work to settle disputes among those who fight or hate. Jesus came to bring peace and wants his peace to penetrate every fiber of our beings.

Reflect: Do you try to settle disputes peacefully? Do you refrain from using words and actions that might cause conflict or harm others? Do you accept others as children of God? Do you pray for peace in your family, school, nation, and world?

1   2   3   4   5

**"Blessed are they who are persecuted for the sake of righteousness,
  for theirs is the kingdom of heaven"** (Matthew 5:10).

We are willing to be persecuted for the sake of righteousness when we do the right thing—even when others ridicule us. Jesus suffered for his convictions and told us we must be willing to pick up the cross of rejection, abuse, and even martyrdom for his sake.

Reflect: Have you suffered for doing the right thing? Can you take criticism and ridicule for not going along with the crowd? Are you willing to share your Catholic and Christian convictions, though others may reject them and you?

1   2   3   4   5

..... Discuss:

❏ In your opinion, people living which Beatitude are least in evidence at your school? In your local community? In the nation?

❏ Which Beatitude is the most difficult for teens to put into practice? Why?

❏ Share a time when you really put a particular Beatitude into practice. What did you feel at the time?

Prayer

The Book of Psalms is *the* prayer book of the Old Testament Scriptures. The Psalms express every sentiment of the human heart. Psalm 8 marvels at the generous God who created such wonderful creatures as humans. Pray this psalm slowly and meditatively, realizing that it is about *you*.

O Lord, our Lord,

how awesome is your name

through all the earth!

You have set your majesty

above the heavens!

What are humans that you are

mindful of them,

mere mortals that you care

for them?

Yet you have made them little

less than a god,

crowned them with glory

and honor.

Psalm 8:2, 5–6

REVIEW

IMPORTANT TERMS TO KNOW

Beatitudes—the heart of Jesus' preaching; they teach us the actions and attitudes that are foundational to the Christian life

freedom—the power rooted in reason and will to act or not to act, to do this or do that, and so to perform deliberate actions on one's own

free will—the power to choose the good over the evil

Magisterium—the official teaching authority in the Church, consisting of the pope and the bishops in communion with him. In the area of morality, the Magisterium has the Christ-given right and duty to proclaim who we are and what we should be before God (see CCC, 2036).

morality—responsible living guided by true human behavior in conformity with God's command to love God and neighbor

CHAPTER SUMMARY

The result of living a moral life is true happiness, or beatitude. In this chapter we learned:

1. Morality is responsible living guided by true human behavior in conformity with God's command to love God and neighbor. We live morally when we are the humans God calls us to be.

2. Human beings have incomparable worth and dignity because we are made in God's image and likeness, have been adopted into the divine family, and are invited to be friends with our Lord and Savior, Jesus Christ.

3. God endows each human with a soul and the abilities to reason, to choose, and to love. With these abilities, we can recognize and freely choose God's will to do good and to avoid evil.

4. Freedom is not a license to do whatever we want to do. Wounded by original sin, human freedom is limited and subject to sin.

5. We are responsible for actions that are voluntary, that is, actions we directly will. Factors like ignorance, fear, force, and habit can limit or destroy our blameworthiness.

6. God wills our eternal happiness. The Beatitudes of Jesus teach us the attitudes of being and ways of acting that will help us achieve happiness God has placed in our heart.

7. Christian morality is responsible Christian living. Its essence is love of God and neighbor as revealed by Jesus Christ.

EXPLORING OUR CATHOLIC FAITH

1. Listening to God's Word

Prayerfully read John 8:31–32. Invite the Spirit to help you understand the meaning of Jesus' words in light of what you learned in this chapter. Discuss your insights with your teacher and others.

2. Understanding the Teachings of the Catholic Church

The Catholic Church teaches that human freedom "attains its perfection when directed toward God, our beatitude" (CCC, 1731). Explain that teaching in your own words. Give concrete examples.

3. Reflecting on Our Catholic Faith

Reflect on this insight into our Catholic belief about human life: "Your life is God's gift to you; what you do with it is your gift to God." In what ways can this insight help you make choices each day? Write your reflections in your journal.

4. Living Our Catholic Faith

Explain whether you agree or disagree with this statement: All freedom has limits. Give examples of how your opinion affects the way you exercise your gift of freedom.

CHAPTER 2

Moral Acts, Passions, and Conscience

"Do to others whatever you would have
them do to you."
MATTHEW 7:12

What Do You Think?

Based on the principles you learned in chapter 1, write "R" if the following are right (moral) or "W" if they are wrong (immoral). Give reasons for your opinion.

_____ 1. While classes are in session, you drive fifteen miles over the speed limit in the school zone of a primary school.

_____ 2. The dean of discipline at your high school searches student lockers for drugs. He does so without getting the students' permission.

_____ 3. An aptitude test reveals that you have tremendous musical ability. However, you refuse to take any music lessons when your mother suggests you do so.

James Patterson and Peter Kim wrote a fascinating book entitled *The Day America Told the Truth*. It reports the following:

❑ Ninety-one percent of the people in the study lie on a regular basis, both at home and at work.

❑ The majority of employees admit to goofing off on the job on the average of seven hours per week.

❑ Half of the workers admit to calling in sick regularly even if they feel well.

❑ Twenty-five percent say they would be willing to leave their families if offered $10 million to do so; 23 percent would be willing to act as prostitutes for a week for that same amount; and 7 percent would agree to murder a stranger.

❑ Only 13 percent hold that all ten commandments are relevant today and binding on people!

KEY TERMS

circumstances

conscience

intention

Magisterium

object

passions

Do these statistics surprise you? Frighten you? Explain.

An antidote to these scary statistics is a healthy dose of people of conscience—those willing to discover and then *do* the right thing. Of course, we all hope that others would recognize us as persons of conscience of whom it could be said: "When you were born, you cried and the world rejoiced. Live your life so when you die, the world cries and you rejoice." This chapter will discuss the morality of human actions, passions, and the meaning of a Christian conscience.

(*Catechism of the Catholic Church,* 1749–1775)

The Sources of Morality

Because we have freedom, we are responsible for our acts and our failures to act. We can judge whether our actions are good or bad by reflecting on three traditional sources of morality. These sources are the object chosen, the end or intention, and the circumstances surrounding the action.

Object Chosen

The object is *what* we do—the act itself. An example of a good act would be something that involves good matter, for example, tutoring a classmate in math. Another example is giving money to Catholic Relief Services to help the victims of an earthquake. "Bad" matter does not conform to our true good. It automatically makes an act evil. For example, trashing a person's reputation contradicts a person's right to a good name; it is evil because *what* we do is wrong.

Objective norms of morality help us judge whether something is good or evil, whether it is in harmony with God's will or is contrary to it. Human reason and the law of conscience enlighten us to these norms.

Some actions by their very nature are always seriously wrong. Examples of such actions are blasphemy, perjury, adultery, and murder. Neither a good intention nor the circumstances surrounding the action can make these evil actions morally good!

Intention

Our intention is the motive or purpose or end for which we choose to do the act. Rooted in our will, our intention answers *why* we acted a certain way. It is a key element in assessing the morality of our actions. For example, you tutor a classmate in math because she is a friend and you want her to do well on the upcoming test. In this example, what is done *and* why it is performed are both good. This act is good.

Our intentions may also be mixed. For example, you may give money to the missions for two reasons. First, you wish to help the poor. But you also want to be praised for your generosity—a less than worthy motive.

Our intention is not always limited to just one act. It can also guide a

Wrong is wrong, even if everyone is doing it. Right is right, even though no one else does it.

series of actions that are working toward the same purpose. For example, a person may be performing a series of acts to rob a bank. The morality of all the person's preliminary acts—which might appear morally acceptable—are tainted because they are motivated by the evil motive of theft.

A major principle of Catholic moral theology centers on the intention behind what we choose to do. This principle is: The end does not justify the means. Stated another way: *A good intention can never turn an intrinsically bad action into a just one.* For example, you may cheat to get a higher grade so you can get into a "good" college. Wanting to go to a good college is certainly a worthy motive; however, cheating is a bad action. A good reason for doing something does not make an evil action morally right. Your good intention may never justify choosing to do something that is by its nature wrong.

The reverse is also true: A bad intention can turn a good act into an evil one. For example, suppose you compliment someone simply because you want to use that person for a letter of recommendation. In this case, you are insincere and are deceitfully using that person to get something you want. You are not treating that person with the respect due him or her. Your motive, or intention, is tainted—though paying a compliment is usually a good act.

Circumstances

Circumstances include the act's consequences and the context within which it is done. The object included the what; and the intention, the why. The circumstances include the *how, who, when,* and *where* of the act.

Circumstances can lessen or increase our blameworthiness for an act. Ignorance, fear, duress, and other psychological and social factors can lessen or nullify our responsibility for our actions. For example, the overwhelming fear of our being sued that kept us from helping a dying victim at an accident scene could greatly diminish our moral responsibility for not helping someone in need when we could have.

The circumstances surrounding an act, however, can never change an act that is by its nature morally evil into a morally good act. For example, a fear of being ridiculed by friends does not justify our speaking racial slurs. Our fear might be understandable, but our cooperation in such acts can never be justified.

In summary, this principle of Christian morality may be stated: For an act to be morally good and acceptable, the object, intention (or end), and circumstances must all be good.

What I do (the object) must be good; why I do it (the intention) and all the surrounding circumstances must also be good. It is wrong to claim an action is good based solely on one's intention or the circumstances and context. We may never choose to do an evil act so good can come from it.

Role of Passions

Passions are our feelings or emotions. They move us to act or not to act in relation to something we feel or imagine to be either good or evil. The most basic passion is love. Love is aroused by and attracted to what is good. Saint Thomas Aquinas teaches that love consists in willing the good of another human being.

Other passions, or emotions, include hatred, joy, sadness, desire, fear, and anger. Passions by themselves are neither good nor evil. Our emotions can help us do good or do bad. For example, anger at racial discrimination can motivate us to do something to combat prejudice. Anger, on the other hand, can contribute to our acting wrongly; for example, striking out at a younger sibling who might be annoying us.

You Decide

Consider the object, intention, and circumstances of each of the following. Decide which of these actions are morally good (G) or morally wrong (W).

_____ 1. You get drunk to escape the tough week you had at school.

_____ 2. Because you did not want them to worry, you tell your folks that you got in at 1:00 A.M. when you actually got home at 2:30 A.M.

_____ 3. Prison officials give an experimental AIDS vaccine to some lifers without their knowledge to find a cure for AIDS.

■ .... Discuss what makes each act right or wrong.

Because of original sin, we have been wounded in our nature, and we do not always use our emotions properly. We need the help of the Holy Spirit to gain mastery of our emotions so we can use our feelings to strengthen our relationship with God and respond lovingly toward others.

(CCC, 1776–1789, 1795–1800, 1802)

Moral Conscience

God gave us a conscience to make and evaluate the moral rightness or wrongness of a concrete act. The *Catechism of the Catholic Church* defines conscience as:

> a judgment of reason whereby the human person recognizes the moral quality of a concrete act that he is going to perform, is in the process of performing, or has already completed. (1778)

The Second Vatican Council tells us that our conscience is the most secret core of who we are; it is the sanctuary where we meet God. In its depths we are alone with God and can hear his call to do good and avoid evil, to live as he, our Abba, our Father, intends us to live.

The Role of Our Conscience

Conscience, then, helps us figure out whether an action or attitude is good or evil, whether it conforms to God's will or contradicts it. Faced with a moral choice, conscience can make a right judgment or an erroneous judgment. We can choose to follow

reason and God's Law or we can choose not to follow them.

Conscience helps us understand the principles of morality and apply them to concrete situations. It helps us judge whether something is good or evil both *before* and *after* we do it. Conscience makes us responsible for our acts. It is conscience that tells us to repent if we have sinned and turned against the Lord and his law of love.

Two Principles of Conscience: Form It and Follow It

Catholic theology has taught two important rules concerning moral decision making:

- ❏ Continually form your conscience.
- ❏ Always follow the certain judgment of your well-formed conscience.

Continual formation of our conscience is a lifelong responsibility that requires a certain degree of *interiority*. This means that we need to develop the ability to quiet down and take a good hard look at our lives before God.

A well-formed conscience is both upright and truthful—two qualities that will bring peace of mind. We must take our responsibility to form our conscience according to the "true good willed by the wisdom" of our Creator. We must take seriously the following:

- ❏ Conscience forms its judgments using human reason, which can help us discover God's goodness and truth.
- ❏ It looks to the Word of God—Jesus—who teaches by his example and his biblical preaching how to live virtuous lives.
- ❏ It looks to Christ's sacrifice on the cross as the prime example of how to love and obey God's will.
- ❏ It seeks guidance from official church teachers and wise and holy people.
- ❏ It is attuned to the gifts of the Holy Spirit which strengthen us to live upright lives.

"**W**hat your conscience says is more important than what your neighbors say."

A continuously well-formed conscience will DECIDE to do the right thing. It will:

D—**ig** out the facts.
E—**xercise** imagination to figure out alternatives and effects.
C—**onsider** the wisdom of others.
I —**mitate** Jesus.
D—**ecide** to do right.
E—**valuate** the decision you made.

Dig Out the Facts. Studying the facts of a proposed action is a prime way to use human reason to discover the truth and the good. Simply by asking questions like *What? Why? Who? Where? When?* and *How?*, we can unearth the moral good or evil in a proposed action. For example, if I find that I have an evil intention (the *why* question), then I know that it would be wrong to perform a particular act. Or if I discover that the *how* is an evil means, then I judge that my proposed action is not morally good.

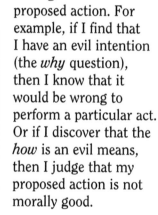

Exercise Imagination. The human spirit includes the faculty of imagination as well as rational thought. Our imagination can help us discover alternative courses to a proposed action. For example, cheating is not the *only* way to pass a test. We can always ask for extra help, join a study group, or ask for an extra day to prepare to take it. These are three morally good alternatives; cheating is not.

Imagination can also help us discover both foreseen and unforeseen effects of a proposed action. Say you are considering gossiping and spreading false rumors about someone. Your sharing of rumors will hurt the person's reputation. But your imagination might also lead you to discover the unforeseen result that you might damage your own name. A friend who hears you gossiping may judge you to be untrustworthy and never confide in you in the future.

Consider the wisdom of other people. As Catholics we look to the Magisterium for moral guidance. We believe that the Holy Spirit guides the Church in knowing and teaching us what is morally good and what is morally evil. Guided by the Holy Spirit, the Magisterium applies both revelation and reason to contemporary issues, pointing out the moral goodness or evil of laws and other social, economic, and political policies.

We also look to others for advice. We turn to the wisdom of our parents, grandparents, and other family members. We seek the advice of priests, those in religious life, and other leaders in our parish community. Saints also serve as our moral guides. We read about the lives of the saints to learn about the decisions they made.

We also recognize and follow the wisdom found in laws that respect the dignity of persons and promote the true good of society. We think of good laws as the written wisdom of those who have gone before us or our contemporary leaders. As we will see in chapter 4, the natural law and the divine law are the two most important sources of forming our conscience correctly.

Sure Guide: The Magisterium • • • • • • •
(CCC, 2030–2040, 2049–2051)

Jesus gave the Church the responsibility to teach truth. The pope and the bishops teach with the authority of Christ. The teaching office of the Church resides in the Magisterium and extends to all elements of doctrine, including moral doctrine.

"The law of God entrusted to the Church is taught to the faithful as the way of life and truth" (CCC, 2037). We have a duty to observe the official teachings of the pope and the bishops who teach lovingly and in a spirit of service. In faith and prayer, we make the Church's teachings part of our daily lives. We form our conscience in light of these teachings because they are meant for our salvation.

Research some of the moral teachings of the Church. List them here.

Imitate Jesus. Jesus is the light of the world. We believe he is the Way, the Light, and the Truth. A close friendship with Jesus Christ is the foundation of our living a moral life and growing in holiness—in our relationship with the Holy Trinity. We can gain insight and courage to choose good and avoid evil by praying to Jesus and asking for the gift of his Holy Spirit.

Decide to do right. Eventually, after you have studied the issue, consulted the wisdom of the Church and other wise people, prayed and looked to Jesus, you must decide. Cooperating with the Holy Spirit's gifts and following the steps taken above, the time will come when we must choose. When it does, we are to follow this rule: "A human being must always obey the certain judgment of his conscience" (CCC, 1800).

Evaluate. Good decisions can strengthen our character and help us increase in the virtues. Saint James writes: "So for one who knows the right thing to do and does not do it, it is a sin" (James 4:17). Conscience helps us evaluate our decisions. If we have done the right thing, we have learned how to decide in similar situations in the future. If we have violated the dictates of our conscience, our conscience convicts us after the fact. It can move us to repent and help us resolve not to sin in the future.

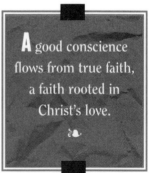

A good conscience flows from true faith, a faith rooted in Christ's love.

Making a Decision

The Word of God offers us this advice:

> Trust in the LORD with all your heart,
>   on your own intelligence rely not;
> In all your ways be mindful of him,
>   and he will make straight your paths.
>
> Proverbs 3:5–6

After reflecting on this passage complete the following:

1. The toughest moral decision for me to deal with usually involves:

2. When it is time for me to make a moral decision, I usually (check all that apply):

    _____ a.   give it little thought

    _____ b.   ask advice

    _____ c.   pray

    _____ d.   agonize over it for a long time

    _____ e.   follow the crowd

    _____ f.   other: _____

Making a Conscientious Decision

How would you resolve this dilemma?

A cashier in a music store at the mall completes the transaction for your purchase of a CD by giving you a ten-dollar bill and some change. She meant to give you a one-dollar bill and some change. She does not notice her mistake.

An Examination of Conscience

An examination of conscience gives each individual an opportunity to examine herself or himself in light of God's Word. Questions, like these, will help you examine your conscience.

Love of God. The Lord says, "You shall love the Lord your God with all your heart" (Mark 12:30). You might ask yourself such questions as:

❏ How am I faithful or unfaithful to God's commandments?

❏ Have I been careful to grow in my understanding of the faith, to hear God's word, to listen to instructions on the faith?

❏ How am I including God in my future?

Love of Neighbor. The Lord says, "[L]ove one another as I love you" (John 15:12). You might ask yourself such questions as:

❏ How am I using the authority that Christ shares with me to build up the reign of God and a better future for the world?

❏ Have I been obedient to my parents? Have I shown respect for my grandparents? How do I respect the people who have the authority and responsibility to care for me?

❏ Do I use my friends and others for my own ends?

❏ Do I do my best to help victims of oppression, people who are homeless, people living in poverty?

Love of Self. Christ our Lord says, "So be perfect, just as your heavenly Father is perfect" (Matthew 5:48). Ask yourself such questions as:

❏ Where is my life going?

❏ What use have I made of time, of health and strength, of the gifts God has given me?

Based on *Rite of Penance*

IMPORTANT TERMS TO KNOW

circumstances—the context and consequences of a moral act—the who, how, when, and where of the act

conscience—"a judgment of reason whereby the human person recognizes the moral quality of a concrete act that he is going to perform, is in the process of performing, or has already completed" (CCC, 1778)

intention—the motive or purpose for a moral act—the why of the act

Magisterium—the official teaching authority in the Church, consisting of the pope and the bishops in communion with him. In the area of morality, the Magisterium has the Christ-given right and duty to proclaim who we are and what we should be before God (see CCC, 2036).

object—the matter of an act: what we do—the what of the act

passions—our feelings or emotions that move us to act or not to act

CHAPTER SUMMARY

In this chapter, we looked at some principles of the Church's moral teaching and Jesus' guidance to learn how to form our conscience and choose correctly. We learned that:

1. The sources of the morality of every human act are the object, the intention, and the circumstances.

2. Some actions are always wrong because they are contrary to our good and God's will.

3. A good intention for an action cannot justify evil means to attain it.

4. Passions are emotions that move us to act or not act in relation to something we feel or imagine to be good or evil. They are neither good nor evil.

5. Conscience is the judgment of reason that enables us to determine the moral quality of a concrete act. It operates before we act, during our act, and after we act.

6. We have the responsibility to form our conscience according to reason and true good willed by God, the Creator. We must always follow our conscience.

7. It is possible for us to form an erroneous conscience. Factors like ignorance, emotion, peer pressure, total self-reliance, a cold heart, and the like, can contribute to an erroneous conscience. Ignorance is not always free of guilt.

8. The Magisterium of the Church has Christ-given authority to teach how to live a moral life in accord with God's will.

EXPLORING OUR CATHOLIC FAITH

1. Listening to God's Word

Read and reflect on Mark 10:17–22. What choice did Jesus offer the young man? How did he respond? What might have been some of the factors that led the young man to his decision?

2. Understanding the Teachings of the Catholic Church

Pope John Paul II taught: "The primary and decisive element for moral judgment is the object of the human act, which establishes whether it is *capable of being ordered to the good and to the ultimate end, which is God*" (*The Splendor of Truth,* 79). Explain what this teaching means.

3. Reflecting on Our Catholic Faith

Someone offered this insight: "Wrong is wrong, even if everyone is doing it. Right is right, even though no one else does it." Does this insight guide you in making moral decisions? Write your thoughts in your journal.

4. Living Our Catholic Faith

Review the DECIDE steps for making a moral decision. Choose a situation that you are facing and apply the steps.

CHAPTER 3

Virtues and Sin

[W]hatever is true, whatever is honorable,
whatever is just, whatever is pure,
whatever is lovely, whatever is gracious,
if there is any excellence and if there is anything
worthy of praise, think about these things.

PHILIPPIANS 4:8

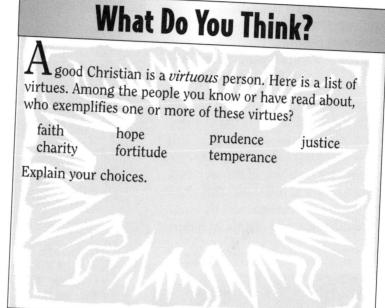
The great baseball Hall-of-Famer Satchel Paige was a colorful observer of the human scene. Because he was black, he was for many years excluded from playing in the major leagues. However, in 1948 he became the oldest rookie in the history of baseball (he was over forty years old) when he joined the Cleveland Indians and helped pitch them to a pennant and a World Series championship. When asked about his uncanny ability to survive in baseball for so long, he offered his six simple rules to live by:

❑ Avoid fried foods which angry up the blood.
❑ If your stomach disputes you, pacify it with cool thoughts.
❑ Keep the juices flowing by jangling around gently as you move.
❑ Go very light on the vices, such as carrying on in society, as the social ramble ain't restful.
❑ Avoid running at all times.
❑ Don't look back; something might be gaining on you.

Add one rule to Satchel's list. Why did you add that rule? Share with your group.

KEY TERMS

capital sins

cardinal virtues

gifts of the Holy Spirit

mortal sin

sin

theological virtues

venial sin

vice

virtue

Satchel Paige (1906?–1982), one of the greatest pitchers in baseball history, joined the Cleveland Indians in 1948 and became the first black pitcher in the American League.

Most people have heard of his last rule. It refers to death, which will eventually catch us all. But note the wisdom of the other five. They tell us to avoid vice and to be moderate in all things.

In fact, in his rules for living, Satchel Paige has restated one of the key, or "cardinal," virtues—temperance. This virtue helps us moderate our appetites for pleasure. It is one of the secrets to living a good and happy life. This chapter will discuss the cardinal and theological virtues, sin, and our social nature.

(*Catechism of the Catholic Church,* 1803–1845)

The Virtues and the Moral Life

There is a saying that goes:
Plant an act; reap a habit.
Plant a habit; reap a virtue or vice.
Plant a virtue or vice; reap a character.
Plant a character; reap a destiny.

God intends us to enjoy a life of eternal happiness. But to reap this destiny, we have to develop virtuous characters and learn to love God, neighbor, and self. We need to make the **virtues** an integral part of our lives.

Virtues are good habits that enable us to choose good and to perform our actions with ease and competence. We acquire the virtues by education and repeated, deliberate acts that form habits. God's grace purifies and elevates these good habits, making it easier for us to do good. Reception of the sacraments and praying to the Holy Spirit for help strengthen virtues and help us avoid **vices.** Vices are bad habits that incline us to do evil.

READING THE BIBLE

Saint Paul warns that if we do not allow the Spirit to live in us, then we will be subject to the temptations of the flesh. Read Galatians 5:19–21 and then list in the space provided the vices Paul mentions.

Which of these vices do you see wreaking havoc in your community or in our nation? Describe the evil effects that vice has on individuals and on the community.

The Cardinal Virtues

Christian tradition recognizes four **cardinal virtues**. The word *cardinal* comes from the Latin word for "hinge." Thus, the four cardinal virtues—prudence, justice, fortitude, and temperance—are the source of all good habits. We acquire them by human reason and personal effort, though God's grace assists us in developing them.

Prudence. Prudence is spiritual common sense, the practical wisdom that helps us discover and bring about proper moral behavior. Saint Thomas Aquinas called prudence "right reason in action." An example of prudence is saying no to *any* offer to take drugs.

Justice. Justice is fairness, giving to God and other people what is due them by right. An example of justice is refusing to spread gossip, thus protecting a person's right to a good name.

Fortitude. Fortitude is the courage to do the right thing, especially in the face of temptation and the emotion of fear. An example of fortitude is refusing to cheat on a test, even though "everyone else" is doing so.

Temperance. Temperance moderates our pleasure-seeking appetites, for example, for food, drink, and sex. An example of temperance is eating healthy food and exercising in moderation to maintain physical fitness.

The Theological Virtues

The cardinal virtues are rooted in the **theological virtues,** which relate us to the Holy Trinity. Three in number—faith, hope, and charity (love)—they have the Triune God as their origin, motive, and object. The theological virtues are the foundation of a Christian moral life.

Faith. Faith enables us to believe in God and what God has revealed through Scripture and the Church. It empowers us to have a personal relationship with Jesus Christ, believe his good news of salvation, and begin a life in communion with the Holy Trinity. Christians must put their faith into action by professing it and sharing it with others. In addition, we must translate our faith into deeds of service.

Hope. Hope gives us the desire for heaven and eternal life. It empowers us to trust in God's promise of salvation. The virtue of hope wards off despair and self-centeredness. It fortifies us to labor for the advancement of God's kingdom, especially by working for justice for the weakest in our midst. Christians gain hope from Christ's Beatitudes. Prayer helps increase it in our lives.

Charity. Charity, or love, is both a virtue and a gift. It enables us to love God above everything for his own sake and to love our neighbor as ourselves for the love of God. Love, or charity, is a share in God's own life. "God is love, and whoever remains in love remains in God and God in him" (1 John 4:16).

Charity is the supreme virtue. It forms and shapes all other virtues, binding them into perfect harmony. "And over all these put on love, that is, the bond of perfection" (Colossians 3:14). The virtue of love is what makes it possible for us to be Christ's instruments of joy, mercy, and peace for others.

Gifts and Fruits of the Holy Spirit

The gifts and fruits of the Holy Spirit help us live as worthy disciples of Jesus Christ, our Lord and Savior. We receive the gifts of the Holy Spirit at baptism to help us be receptive to God's grace working in our lives. Drawing on Isaiah 11:1–2 and traditions, the Church lists seven gifts bestowed on us through the Spirit. They are wisdom, understanding, counsel, strength, knowledge, piety, and fear of the Lord.

"The *fruits* of the Spirit are perfections that the Holy Spirit forms in us as the first fruits of eternal glory" (CCC, 1832). Church Tradition lists nine of these fruits. They are love, joy, peace, patience, kindness, generosity, gentleness, faithfulness, and self-control (see Galatians 5:22–23).

(CCC, 1846–1876)

Sin

The main point of the Gospel is to reveal God's mercy to sinners through Jesus Christ. However, if we do not convert and admit that we are sinners, then we will not be open to the forgiving touch of the Divine Physician. Our consciences can tell the truth

Saint Paul teaches, "So faith, hope, love remain, these three; but the greatest of these is love" (1 Corinthians 13:13). Paul describes several dimensions of love in the verses that precede 13:13. Read Paul's description of the dimensions of love. Why does Paul call love the greatest?

What do you think?

What would happen in an individual's life and in the life of a community if it was built on "love" as Paul describes it?

about our sinful behavior and convince us to turn to our Lord who will surely save us. Thus, the bad news of sin in our lives becomes the good news of Jesus saving us by forgiving our sins.

What is sin? "Sin is an offense against reason, truth, and right conscience; it is failure in genuine love for God and neighbor caused by a perverse attachment to certain goods" (CCC, 1849).

Sin is an offense against God, a choosing of self over God, a disobedient revolt against God's love.

There are different ways to list sins, for example, those that are directed against God, neighbor, and self. One categorization lists those of the spirit versus those of the flesh. Another classifies sins according to those of thought, word, deed, or failure to act.

Yet another category distinguishes between original sin and personal sin. Finally, Church Tradition has looked to the seriousness of sins—venial sin and mortal sin.

Original and Personal Sin

Original sin explains the disharmonious condition into which all of us are born. Pope Paul VI described it this way:

It is human nature so fallen, stripped of the grace that clothed it, injured in its own natural powers and subjected to the dominion of death . . .

Credo of the People of God, 16

We inherit this condition from our first parents. Confirming the existence of original sin is easy. We simply need to look at the evil in the world around us: poverty, prejudice, war, greed, sensual appetites out of control. We need only look within our own hearts: our anger, our inclination to do evil, our failure to keep our good resolutions, and the like. By our own efforts, we are powerless to overcome the effects of original sin. This is why we need our Savior—Jesus Christ—and the graces of the Holy Spirit.

Personal sin is *actual* sin that we ourselves freely commit. It is any free and deliberate act, word, thought, or desire that turns us away from God's law to love. It either weakens (venial sin) or kills (mortal sin) our relationship with God. Sin can also produce social and institutional structures that are contrary to God's will. These "structures of sin" result from personal sin. They cause an evil society and help lead people to sin.

Mortal Sin

Mortal sin gravely violates God's Law. The three conditions of grave matter, full knowledge, and complete consent of the will must be present for a person to sin mortally.

Grave matter. The moral object must be of such a nature that it destroys love in us and totally turns us away from God. The Ten Commandments specify what is grave matter and correspond to what Jesus said to the wealthy young man (see Mark 10:19).

Full knowledge. For a person to commit mortal sin, not only must the matter be grave, but the person must fully know that the act is seriously wrong and in opposition to God's Law. Unintentional ignorance can reduce or even remove the blameworthiness of a grave offense.

Complete consent. Mortal sin also "implies a consent sufficiently deliberate to be a personal choice" (CCC, 1859). Factors like strong emotions, external force, or psychological sickness can reduce the voluntary character of one's acts. "Feigned ignorance and hardness of heart (see Mark 3:5–6 and Luke 16:19–31) do not diminish, but rather increase, the voluntary character of a sin" (CCC, 1859).

Humans can and do sin mortally. The possibility of sinning mortally flows from our freedom. We have the freedom to choose; we have the freedom to love or not to love. We have the freedom to turn our backs on God. The effects of sinning mortally include the loss of charity and sanctifying grace. If not repented and forgiven, mortal sin excludes us from God's kingdom and merits for us eternal loss.

If we should sin mortally, we should repent of our sin immediately and ask for God's forgiveness, which is always offered to us. For Catholics, the sacrament of Penance is the normal means Christ left us to have our mortal sins forgiven.

Venial Sin

One commits venial sin when grave matter, full knowledge, or complete consent are not involved. (See CCC, 1862.)

Venial sin does not kill our friendship with God. It does not drive out love or sanctifying grace nor deprive us of eternal happiness in heaven, but merits temporal punishment. Venial sin weakens love in us, slows us in the practice of the virtues, and may dispose us little by little to commit mortal sin.

Venial sin is reparable by our love— by our love of God and neighbor. The Church, however, encourages us to confess our venial sins in the sacrament of Penance as a spiritual practice to grow in holiness. However, we are not required to do so. We can ask God to forgive them in the penitential rite at Mass or in private prayer. We can also offer up some work of self-denial to counteract the self-centered tendencies that cause us to sin.

Sin Increases

The danger with sin is that it is "addictive." It can become habit-forming, and we can become attached to it. Sin can easily become repetitive so that we form bad habits known as vices. A vice is a bad habit that inclines us to do evil and avoid doing good.

Certain of these vices, which are so deadly, are known as **capital sins.** They are pride, envy, anger, sloth, greed, gluttony, and lust.

These seven sins have one thing in common: they can lead us to sin mortally. For example, sloth—spiritual laziness—may keep us from worshiping God on Sunday; because of our greed we can turn ourselves into totally selfish people. Such selfishness drives out God's love.

Sin also increases when we cooperate with others in their sins; for example, we praise their evil acts, fail to deter others from sinning when we could, or even protect evildoers.

Q&A

Does God forgive all sin?

God always forgives us and loves us immensely. But we need to respond to that love. We need to not only turn from our sins but also ask for God's mercy. And God will forgive us!

All sin is forgivable for the one who repents of it and turns to God for his mercy. However, Scripture tells us of one unforgivable sin, the so-called sin against the Holy Spirit. (See Mark 3:29.)

The Church interprets this passage this way: The one unforgivable sin is the refusal to accept God's gift of mercy through repentance. If a person freely rejects forgiveness and the gift of salvation offered by the Holy Spirit, then God does not force his love on the person. Such a person has a "hard heart" that refuses to accept God's love.

(CCC, 1877–1948)

Our Social Nature: A Key Ingredient to Moral Living

Humans, by nature, are called to live in society. Humans are social beings who live with and for others. As individuals and as a human community, God calls us into union with the Holy Trinity, a true communion of love. We become truly human and reach our potential by serving and dialoguing with others. Love of neighbor is inseparable from the love of God.

The Person and Society

Societies include personal ones like the family, voluntary organizations like neighborhood groups, and political institutions like the state. They all have one thing in common: the human person must always "be the beginning, the subject and the object of every social organization" (*Pastoral Constitution on the Church in the Modern World*, 25).

A major role of any society is to promote virtue among its members, recognizing individuals as ends in themselves and not as a means. A good society inspires individuals to inner conversion and a sense of service to others. Christians recognize that love is the basis of any good society. This supreme virtue helps us respect others as individuals of worth and gives us God's strength to treat them justly and selflessly. Christians see a tight link between the Gospel and a just society.

The following themes emerge from our social nature. They name ways that

The left column lists five sins that neither respect the dignity of people nor promote the good of society. Match each sin named by checking the biblical references given.

_____ 1. The cry of the foreigner, widow, and orphan

A. Exodus 3:7–10

_____ 2. The blood of Abel

B. Deuteronomy 24:14–15; James 5:4

_____ 3. Sin of the Sodomites

C. Genesis 4:10

_____ 4. Injustice to the wage earner

D. Genesis 18:20

_____ 5. Cry of the oppressed Israelites

E. Exodus 22:20–22

Evil does exist in our world. There are evil actions of individuals and communities that do not promote a good society. What evil actions are you aware of? List them here. What can the Church do to work against those evils? What can your parish do? What can your family do? What can you do with your friends? What can you do?

societies should relate to the individual and the ways individuals should relate to societies.

The Principle of Subsidiarity. Societies should exist to benefit the individual. Thus, the principle of **subsidiarity** holds that a larger social unit should not take over the functions of a smaller group if the smaller unit can achieve for itself the common good. For example, the state should not intrude into the family by dictating how parents should raise their children or what religious values they should teach. Taking into consideration the common good, larger societal units should support smaller organizations and coordinate their functions with the rest of society.

The Virtue of Solidarity. The principle of **solidarity** outlaws collectivist forms of government (like communism) because they make individual persons subordinate to the state. Governments must develop and protect conditions that guarantee the exercise of freedom. It also requires that leaders share their authority with those they serve, just as God shares his authority with humans. Finally, this principle limits state intervention and works to bring peace between individuals, societies, and nations.

Respect for True Authority. Authority is a quality possessed by persons or institutions to make laws, fully expecting others to obey them. Authority's ultimate source is God.

This is why we have a duty to respect those who legitimately hold positions of authority, and why those in authority must maintain order and work for the common good through just, moral, and equitable laws.

Citizens have the fundamental right to choose their political rulers.

Centrality of the Common Good. Vatican II defines the **common good** as "the sum total of social conditions which allow people, either as groups or as individuals, to reach their fulfillment more fully and more easily" (*Pastoral Constitution on the Church in the Modern World*, 26).

The common good involves three essential elements:

❑ First, individuals and societies must respect the basic, inalienable rights of each person.

❑ Second, society and individuals must promote the social well-being and development of various social groups.

❑ Third, for the first two elements to happen, the common good requires peace, the necessary condition of a stable and secure environment brought out by a just order. Thus, those in authority should use moral means to secure a peaceful society, including the right to personal and national defense.

Within nations, government officials have a primary task of promoting the common good of the civil society, the individuals in it, and the various organizations that comprise the nation.

We belong not only to local and national societies, but to the world community as well. Thus, nations should organize to promote the common good for all humans. They should support human progress and just development by never subordinating the individual to the state. Finally, they should exercise the virtues of truth, justice, and love as the basis for international cooperation.

Because we are social beings, we must take an active part in our social groups, especially exercising responsibility in the associations to which we directly belong. Thus, a teen can work for a family's common good by cooperating with siblings, helping with chores, and obeying the moral rules of parents. Similarly, an employee should give a full day's work for a full day's pay. And, after studying the various issues, citizens must conscientiously vote for candidates they judge to be the best promoters of the common good.

Christians will take a very active role in the public arena to guarantee the basic human rights for all people. By definition, a Christian shows concern for others. And a primary way to manifest that concern is to be actively involved in the social life of the groups to which he or she belongs.

Social Justice

The Church has a rich and forward-looking body of social justice teaching. It promotes social justice which works for the conditions that allow groups and individuals to obtain their just due, according to their nature or vocation in life. We conclude this chapter with four fundamental truths that flow from our being made in God's image.

We must respect each human person. God makes each person to his image and likeness from the first moment of conception. We can know and love God, freely shape our lives, and love and develop friendships with others. We are social beings who are friends of Jesus and children of an incredibly loving Father. Jesus taught us that *every* human person is our neighbor, another self. He taught us to respect all people, forgiving those who have hurt us— loving our enemies. He commanded us to respect in a special way the down-trodden and the poor, serving them and treating them like other Christs.

We are essentially equal. We all share the same human nature, have a common destiny, and possess an inherent dignity. We all have basic God-given rights. Discrimination based on sex, race, color, language, ethnicity, national origin, socioeconomic status, or religion is contrary to God's loving plan for us.

We are to develop our gifts and share them with others. Although we all have equal dignity, God endows us with a variety of gifts and talents. These differences are part of God's plan. The Lord expects us to develop and then share our gifts and talents with others. Those who have many gifts must especially use them for the benefit of others. Those who have used these gifts and have acquired wealth and access to education must lead the fight against unjust inequalities, especially those economic and social conditions that destroy justice, harm human dignity, and disrupt peace.

Human and Christian brotherhood and sisterhood require solidarity. Solidarity, which is known as friendship or social charity, is a Christian virtue. It is the habit that enables us to work to share material goods and, more importantly, spiritual goods with others. Solidarity is especially at work when we fulfill the needs of people who are weak, defenseless, and living in poverty.

We exist in a network of relationships; we are one family under God. The virtue of solidarity inspires cooperation and sharing—the poor among themselves, the wealthy and those in poverty, employees and employers, and various national and population groups. As Christians, we cannot escape the call to take care of each other.

Dorothy Day (1897–1980) was an American journalist and cofounder of the Catholic Workers, a Roman Catholic movement that promotes peace, charity, and nonviolent social change.

Prayer

The Spirit has been given to us to teach us and strengthen us to live as children of God. Trusting in God's love, we pray:

Lord God,
creator and ruler of your
   kingdom of light,
in your great love for this world
you gave up your only Son
for our salvation.
His cross has redeemed us,
his death has given us life,
his resurrection has raised us to
   glory.
Through him we ask you
to be always present among your
   family.
Teach us to be reverent in the
   presence of your glory;
fill our hearts with faith,
our days with good works,
our lives with your love;
may your truth be on our lips
and your wisdom in all our
   actions,
that we may receive the reward
   of everlasting life.

We ask this through Christ our
   Lord.
Amen.

Rite of Penance

IMPORTANT TERMS TO KNOW

capital sins—pride, envy, anger, sloth, greed, gluttony, and lust; the principal sinful tendencies of humans subject to the effects of original sin

cardinal virtues—prudence, justice, fortitude, and temperance

gifts of the Holy Spirit—wisdom, understanding, counsel, strength, knowledge, piety, and fear of the Lord

mortal sin—personal sin that totally rejects God and alienates one from him, causing a loss of love and sanctifying grace; it involves grave matter, full knowledge, and complete consent

sin—"an offense against reason, truth, and right conscience; it is a failure in genuine love for God and neighbor" (CCC, 1849)

theological virtues—faith, hope, and charity; bestowed at baptism, these virtues have their origin and goal in God by relating us to the Holy Trinity

venial sin—personal sin that weakens but does not kill our relationship with God

vice—a bad habit that inclines us to do evil and avoid good

virtue—a good habit that enables us to do good

CHAPTER SUMMARY

1. The virtues are good habits that help us choose the good and act with ease and competence. The theological virtues are faith, hope, and charity and are rooted in God and orient us to him. The cardinal virtues are the hinge virtues of prudence, justice, fortitude, and temperance.

2. The gifts and fruits of the Holy Spirit help us live as the Lord's disciples.

3. Sin is an offense against God, a disobedient revolt against his love. Original sin, the fallen condition into which all humans are born, makes us prone to sin. Personal sin is that which individuals personally commit. Sinful social structures help sin to increase and entice people to turn their backs on God's love.

4. Mortal sin is a grave violation of God's Law. It involves grave, or very serious matter, full knowledge, and complete consent. Venial sin is a partial rejection of God. It does not destroy love in us but weakens it. Venial sin may dispose us to sin seriously in the future.

5. The capital sins of pride, envy, anger, sloth, greed, gluttony, and lust are vices or bad habits that can lead us to sin mortally.

6. We are social beings who must work together to promote the common good. The principle of subsidiarity regulates how larger social units relate to smaller ones. The virtue of solidarity calls us to take care of each other because we are all children of God.

EXPLORING OUR CATHOLIC FAITH

1. Listening to God's Word

The Book of Proverbs contains many maxims, or short, pointed sentences that guide us in living moral lives. Read Proverbs 14. What do the proverbs in this chapter tell us about living a moral life?

2. Understanding the Teachings of the Catholic Church

The bishops at the Second Vatican Council taught that we can neither live nor develop our gifts if we do not enter into relationships with others. Using the concepts learned in this chapter, explain the meaning of this teaching.

3. Reflecting on Our Catholic Faith

Saint John Vianney (1786–1859) shares this insight into the moral life: "Virtue demands courage, constant effort, and, above all, help from on high." In what ways does this help you meet the demands of living a moral life? Write your insights in your journal.

4. Living Our Catholic Faith

List ways you can live the teaching that states showing respect for another person is showing respect for Christ and for oneself.

CHAPTER 4

Law, Grace, Church

[B]e fervent in spirit, serve the Lord.
Rejoice in hope, endure in affliction,
persevere in prayer. Contribute to the needs
of the holy ones, exercise hospitality.

ROMANS 12:11–13

What Do You Think?

$\mathbf{M}$atch the terms below with the descriptions given:

_____ 1. A rule of conduct legislated by the competent authority for the sake of the common good

_____ 2. The light of understanding placed in us by God

_____ 3. A wonderful statement of the New Law (law of the Gospel)

_____ 4. God's free and undeserved help; participation in God's own life

_____ 5. An excellent summary of the Old Law

A. grace

B. Sermon on the Mount

C. law

D. Ten Commandments

E. natural law

A famous, oft-quoted description of success comes from the American essayist Ralph Waldo Emerson. As you read his description, consider whether you agree or disagree with his examples.

What is success?
To laugh often and much;
To win the respect of intelligent people
    and the affection of children;
To earn the appreciation of honest critics
    and endure the betrayal of false friends;
To appreciate beauty;
To find the best in others;
To leave the world a bit better,
    whether by a healthy child, a garden patch
    or a redeemed social condition;
To know even one life has breathed easier
    because you have lived;
This is to have succeeded.

Everyone has an idea about what a successful life is. How about you? What does being a successful person mean for you?

KEY TERMS

Decalogue

grace

justification

merit

natural law

precepts of the Church

sanctifying grace

Mother Teresa (1910–1997), Roman Catholic nun and 1979 Nobel Peace Prize winner, is remembered as the "saint of the gutters." In 1950 she founded a religious order in Calcutta, India, called the Missionaries of Charity.

Most would find wisdom in Emerson's observations. Yet, we might ask even a better question: What would Jesus of Nazareth, the Christ, see as a successful life? One of his famous twentieth-century disciples, Mother Teresa of Calcutta, responded that she never worried about success, only whether she was faithful. A good answer! Being faithful to Christ Jesus is the key to a successful . . . and moral . . . and happy life.

In this chapter we will examine several ways God assists us in living faithful, loving, moral Christian lives: law, justification and grace, the guidance of the Church, the precepts of the Church, and the Ten Commandments.

(Catechism of the Catholic Church, 1949–1986)

The Moral Law

God calls us to be happy with him, but sin holds us back. We need God's own help to be rescued, to reach our heavenly goal. Thankfully, Christ Jesus saves us by his many graces. Furthermore, the Holy Spirit guides us in living the moral law.

The moral law is a major help on the road to living a good life. It is God's fatherly instruction, pointing out good and evil, on how to live to attain union with the Holy Trinity in heaven. Saint Thomas Aquinas defined law as a reasonable regulation issued by the proper authority for the common good. All law finds its roots in the moral law of God's providence, that is, God's wisdom, power, and goodness.

Jesus Christ is the fullness and source of unity of the moral law. He is the purpose of the law because he teaches and gives us God's justice. The four interrelated expressions of the moral law are the *eternal law,* which finds its source in God, the author of all law; the *natural law*; *revealed law,* consisting of the Old Law and the law of the Gospel; and *civil and church laws*.

Natural Law

"The natural law is nothing other than the light of understanding placed in us by God; through it we know what we must do and what we must avoid. God has given this light or law at the creation" (CCC, 1955. See Saint Thomas Aquinas, On the Ten Commandments I.).

We have been created in the image and likeness of God. The natural law is our share in God's wisdom and goodness. It expresses the dignity of the human person and serves as the basis of our fundamental rights and duties. It is the foundation of all moral rules and civil laws. Because God created us with a rational mind, we can discover the truth of the natural law.

While humans have applied the natural law differently according to various cultures, the general precepts of the natural law are *universal, permanent,* and *unchanging*. As a result, it is binding on all people, everywhere, for all time.

The natural law is the source of the rules of morality and the basis of various civil laws. It is the very foundation for humans living together in harmony. For example, note the moral chaos and societal cancer that result when individuals or societies violate the natural law by permitting the killing of innocent human beings.

In Your Opinion

● ●

Laws . . . Laws . . . Laws

Saint Thomas Aquinas (c. 1225–1274) teaches that good laws are reasonable rules, legislated by proper authority, for the benefit of the common good. Read over these rules and laws. Check whether you think each is a good law or rule (column 1) or a bad one (column 2). Check column 3 if you are not sure.

Law			
Drivers should observe all stop signs.	1	2	3
All homeowners must pay taxes to support the local public schools.	1	2	3
No student can take *any* medication without the school nurse dispensing it.	1	2	3
Males *and* females of the proper age and in good health must submit to a draft in time of war.	1	2	3
Students bringing weapons to school will be expelled.	1	2	3
Catholics must participate in Mass every Sunday.	1	2	3
With her doctor's agreement, a woman can have an abortion on demand.	1	2	3

.... Discuss:

Share reasons for your choices.

For those laws and rules that you thought were bad, what change in the wording of the law could garner your support?

What is the most ridiculous law or rule that has ever directly affected you?

What makes for a bad law or rule?

Revealed Law

Because of original sin, the ability of our intellect is weakened. Sometimes we have difficulty discerning the natural law. However, God has revealed the precepts of the moral law to us. The first stage of this revelation is the Law of Moses, summarized in the Ten Commandments, or Decalogue, which contain the major precepts of the natural law. This first stage of revelation was a preparation for the New Law of the Gospel, the Law of Christ, which would be written in a new and defining way on the human heart.

The Old Law. The Mosaic Law spells out the many moral truths that human reason can discover. God revealed them because humans had failed to read them in their hearts. The Decalogue shows us what to do and what to avoid. Its chief purpose is both to reveal and denounce sin, what is contrary to love of God, neighbor, and self.

The New Law. The Law of Moses prepares for the Gospel of Jesus Christ, the New Law. "The New Law is the grace of the Holy Spirit received by faith in Christ, operating through charity" (CCC, 1983).

New Testament teachings from the Sermon on the Mount and in the apostolic teachings (Romans 12–15, 1 Corinthians 12–13, Colossians 3–4, and Ephesians 4–5) reveal that the New Law is a *law of love*. It enables us to put into action the Holy Spirit's gift of love. The New Law is also a *law of grace* that strengthens us to love obediently, through faith and the sacramental graces. Finally, it is a *law of freedom*, empowering us to act as God's children and friends of the Lord who can hear and then respond to the inner call to love.

The New Law is also called the law of the Gospel. It is the work of Christ, who most perfectly reveals it in the Sermon on the Mount. It is also the work and grace of the Holy Spirit who works within our hearts by writing the law of love on our hearts, reforming us to imitate our heavenly Father more closely. We can summarize the law of the Gospel this way: "Do to others whatever you would have them do to you" (Matthew 7:12); and "[L]ove one another as I love you" (John 15:12).

(*CCC*, 1987–2029)

Grace and Justification

We live God's laws and a moral life because God's grace has "justified" us. **Grace** is God's favor—a sharing in the very life and love of God and his free and undeserved help. **Justification** is the Holy Spirit's grace that cleanses us from our sins through faith in Jesus Christ and Baptism. It includes the remission of sins, sanctification, and the renewal of our inner self.

Justification

Justification imparts to us God's righteousness. It unites us to Jesus' Paschal mystery, his saving Passion and Resurrection, and makes us sharers in the life of the Holy Trinity. Within the community of the Church, which is Christ's Body, the Spirit teaches us to repent of our sins and accept Jesus into our lives.

We are justified before God because of Jesus' death on the cross. His great sacrifice opened the storehouse of God's graces. Without these graces, we are helpless in developing spiritually. The Spirit teaches us to repent of our sins and accept Jesus into our lives. If we freely cooperate with God's grace and listen to the inner call of the Holy Spirit, we can grow in holiness.

The grace of justification is necessary for living a moral life because it forgives our sins and brings about internal renewal. It bestows the gifts of faith, hope, and charity—the virtues that help us obey God's will.

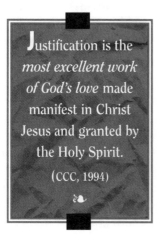

Justification is the *most excellent work of God's love* made manifest in Christ Jesus and granted by the Holy Spirit.

(CCC, 1994)

Grace

The word *grace* comes from the Latin word *gratia,* meaning "gift." We call God's free gift of himself and his help to us **grace.** God's grace helps us live as children of God, a life of intimacy with the Holy Trinity.

God has implanted in our hearts a great desire to know the truth and to do good—to know, love, and serve him. These yearnings of our heart, our very being, are signs that God has begun the work of grace by preparing for, preceding, and gently calling forth our free response to his love.

God in Your Life

The Tradition of the Church distinguishes several types of graces: *sanctifying grace,* or habitual grace, which is the gratuitous gift of God's life to us; *actual graces,* which are God's special gifts that help us convert from sin or help us live a Christ-like life once we have converted; *sacramental graces,* which are gifts that flow from particular sacraments; *charisms,* which are special graces the Holy Spirit bestows on individual Christians to help the Church grow; *graces of state,* which are special divine helps that go with particular ministries within the Church.

These many names the Tradition of the Church gives to grace help us understand the many ways God is present and active in our lives. How does this help you understand your relationship to God?

Grace adopts us into the divine family, making us partakers of the life of the Holy Trinity. Because it heals us of sin and restores us to holiness, we call this grace **sanctifying grace.** Infused into our soul by the Holy Spirit, sanctifying grace makes us heirs to heaven and empowers us to live as God's children.

It enables us to call God "Abba," unites us to Jesus, and gives us the life of the Holy Spirit.

The sacrament of Baptism confers this supernatural gift on us, a gift that we cannot earn. Its bestowal depends totally on God's gracious love for us. Another term for sanctifying grace is *habitual grace,* because it permanently disposes us to live like God.

We need the gift of faith to recognize grace working in our lives. Faith and trust in God's mercy can give us the inner vision to see God's blessings in our lives and in those of others.

Merit and Holiness

Merit and holiness are closely related to justification and grace. Both are possible because of God's initiative and love for us.

Merit. Merit is something owed us because of our good deeds. But in reality, God does not owe us anything. God has given us everything—life, salvation, adoption into the divine family. So, how can we speak of meriting anything in relationship to God?

In his great wisdom and love, God has enabled us to share in his work of grace. Because God chose us to be his special children, he will reward us with eternal life. However, we must cooperate with the various graces the Spirit gives us to live loving and holy lives to "merit" that reward.

Merit, then, is first of all associated with the grace of God; and second, with our cooperation with God. Without the first, there is no merit. We cannot merit the grace of conversion, which is our initial turning toward God. However, we can and must cooperate with this initial grace.

With the Holy Spirit's help, we can also "merit" for ourselves and others certain blessings and graces needed for living our life as children of God here on earth and for attaining eternal life in heaven. Because God's love, generosity, and providence also extend to our well-being on earth, we can also merit certain earthly, or temporal, goods.

Christ Jesus' love is the source of all merit before God. God gives us gifts *through* his Son, whose love has won us everything. Jesus is the key to understanding the concepts of merit, justification, and grace. If we allow Christ Jesus to live in us through the power of the Holy Spirit and his gift of sanctifying grace, then the Lord and his Holy Spirit will make us holy and merit for us eternal life before our loving, merciful, Triune God.

Holiness. Living a life of holiness involves striving to live as children of God, in whose image and likeness we have been created. God calls *everyone* to be holy. The Church teaches "that all Christians in any state or walk of life are called to the fullness of Christian life and to the perfection of love . . ." (*Dogmatic Constitution on the Church,* 40).

The goal of our life of holiness is full union with the Holy Trinity through our union with Christ. The way of Christ's cross is the way to holiness, the perfection of love. Works of self-denial, penance, and mortification serve as the way to holiness. Stated another way, the motto "No cross, no crown" reveals that growth in our life of holiness involves some pain, that is, self-denial for the sake of Christ and others.

We prayerfully trust that God will give us the strength to remain in love up to our death so we may one day gain the promised eternal reward of heaven.

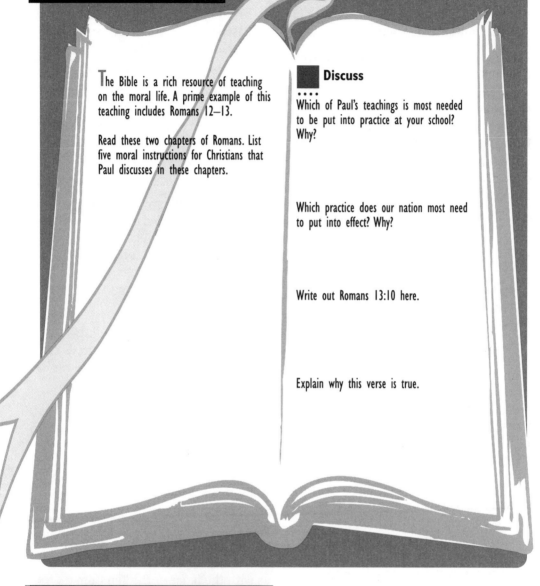

The Bible is a rich resource of teaching on the moral life. A prime example of this teaching includes Romans 12–13.

Read these two chapters of Romans. List five moral instructions for Christians that Paul discusses in these chapters.

Discuss

....

Which of Paul's teachings is most needed to be put into practice at your school? Why?

Which practice does our nation most need to put into effect? Why?

Write out Romans 13:10 here.

Explain why this verse is true.

(CCC, 2030–2082)

The Church: Mother and Teacher

As followers of the Lord Jesus, we fulfill our vocation to live a life of holiness in his Body, the Church. We receive the Word of God, which contains Christ's law of love within the Church. We celebrate the sacraments and receive their graces as members of the Church. We learn how to be holy from the many saints in the Christian community, especially from the Blessed Mother.

We can speak of our living a moral life as spiritual worship. The liturgy and sacraments of the Church are a wonderful source of strength to support us in living Christlike, moral lives. The Eucharist—the source and summit of Christian life—is a source of spiritual power to do right.

Consider all the good we do when we live holy and moral lives joined to Christ in the Eucharist. First, we actually worship God when we sacrifice by living a good life. Second, we witness to our Christian faith and draw others to Christ, thus building up Christ's Body. Third, by cooperating with the Holy Spirit, living in and working through us, we help him in the work of establishing his kingdom.

The Precepts of the Church

The Church community sees a strong connection between celebrating the liturgy, praying, and living the moral life. The precepts of the Church are minimum standards that good Catholics will observe to live the Christian life in the Catholic community. They help nurture us on our spiritual journey and strengthen us to live as responsible Christians. The precepts of the Church are:

❏ "You shall attend Mass on Sundays and holy days of obligation." This precept requires the faithful to participate in the eucharistic celebration when the Christian community gathers together on the day commemorating the Resurrection of the Lord.

❏ "You shall confess your sins at least once a year." This precept ensures preparation for the Eucharist by the reception of the sacrament Penance, which continues Baptism's work of conversion and forgiveness.

❏ "You shall humbly receive your Creator in Holy Communion at least during the Easter season." This precept guarantees as a minimum the reception of the Lord's Body and Blood in connection with the Paschal feasts, the origin and center of the Christian liturgy.

❏ "You shall keep holy the holy days of obligation." This precept completes the Sunday observance by participation in the principal liturgical feasts which honor the mysteries of the Lord, the Virgin Mary, and the saints.

❏ "You shall observe the prescribed days of fasting and abstinence." This precept ensures the times of ascesis and penance which prepare us for the liturgical feasts; they help us acquire mastery over our instincts and freedom of heart.

❏ The faithful also have the duty of providing for the material needs of the Church, each according to his or her abilities.

The Ten Commandments

Sociological studies report that school children are happier when their playgrounds have fences around them. Fences provide a sense of security, not imprisonment, to children, making them freer to play. God has provided us with the fence of the Ten Commandments, or Decalogue, to help us live a moral life. Rather than imprison us with meaningless rules and regulations, the commandments free us to be the children of God we are meant to be.

We find the Decalogue in the Old Testament in the books of Exodus and Deuteronomy. These biblical books reveal how God sealed his covenant of love with the Israelites by giving them the Law and the Ten Commandments.

They reveal his holy will for those he called to be his own children and a special witness to humanity. A reflection on the covenant nature of the commandments helps us see that when we keep them, we are returning our love to a loving God who calls and sustains us.

We are also obeying our Lord Jesus, who told us to keep the commandments (for example, in Matthew 19:16–19). Jesus taught us how to keep the inner spirit of the Law, revealing to us how the Holy Spirit is at work in the Law. Jesus summarized the Law and the commandments this way: Love God with all your heart, soul, and mind, and love your neighbor as yourself (see Matthew 22:37–40).

From the days of the apostles, the Church has always taught the centrality of the commandments in living a moral life. Each of the commandments is linked with the others, thus uniting the love of God with the love of neighbor. Later church councils, for example, the Council of Trent (1542–1549) and the Second Vatican Council (1962–1965) have clearly taught that we have a serious obligation to keep the commandments. The commandments teach us the way to truth, outline our basic duties as humans, and, therefore, protect our fundamental human rights. This is why obeying them is a serious duty.

The Ten Commandments bind all people, in all places, at all times. God has written them on our hearts. And because he is a good and loving God, he gives us the graces that are necessary to obey them on our journey to eternal life. The last six chapters of this book will look at the specific values in each commandment and discuss some of the actions and attitudes that violate them.

What the Documents Say

[T]he faithful, for their part, are obliged to submit to their bishops' decision, made in the name of Christ, in matters of faith and morals, and to adhere to it with a ready and respectful allegiance of mind.

Dogmatic Constitution on the Church, 25

Discuss: What is the importance of this teaching in guiding you in making moral decisions? Where can you find the teachings of the Church on moral issues?

The Ten Commandments

I	I am the LORD, your God: you shall not have strange gods before me.
II	You shall not take the name of the LORD your God in vain.
III	Remember to keep holy the LORD's day.
IV	Honor your father and your mother.
V	You shall not kill.
VI	You shall not commit adultery.
VII	You shall not steal.
VIII	You shall not bear false witness against your neighbor.
IX	You shall not covet your neighbor's wife.
X	You shall not covet your neighbor's goods.

REVIEW

IMPORTANT TERMS TO KNOW

Decalogue—means "ten words," and is another term used for the Ten Commandments

grace—the free and supernatural gift of God's life and friendship. God's favor, his free and undeserved help.

justification—the Holy Spirit's grace that cleanses us from our sins through faith in Jesus Christ and baptism; justification makes us right with God

merit—"the *recompense owed* by a community or a society for the action of one of its members, experienced either as beneficial or harmful, deserving reward or punishment. . . . With regard to God, there is no strict right to any merit on the part of man" (CCC, 2006, 2007).

natural law—the light of under-standing implanted by God in us so we can discover what we must do and what we must avoid; God's plan written in the very way he made things. Reason can help us discover God's eternal law and learn what good must be done and what evil must be avoided

precepts of the Church—minimal obligations that flow from being a member of the Catholic faith community, for example, Mass attendance on Sundays and holy days of obligation, fasting and abstaining on designated days, and supporting the local and worldwide Church

sanctifying grace—the gift of God that makes us holy, permanently disposing us to live like God

CHAPTER SUMMARY

1. The moral law, rooted in God, the author of all law, guides us in responsible, Christian living.

2. The natural law is the light of understanding that God placed in us so we can discover what is right and wrong.

3. The New Law of the Gospel of Jesus Christ is a law of love, a work of grace and the Holy Spirit.

4. The Holy Spirit justifies us by cleansing us of our sins through faith in Christ Jesus and Baptism. Justification is necessary for the forgiveness of sins and internal renewal. Justification flows from grace.

5. Sanctifying or habitual grace is God's favor, his free and undeserved help. It heals us of sin and makes us holy.

6. In his goodness and generosity, God has merited us eternal life. God allows us to cooperate with his gift of salvation. Thus, our good works can earn merit for us and others. However, this can only be done through Jesus Christ, the source of all merit.

7. God calls everyone to holiness.

8. The Church's Magisterium is a sure guide for learning about right and wrong. Because the pope and bishops teach with Christ's authority, we must adhere to their doctrines in the areas of faith and morals.

9. The Ten Commandments spell out the precepts of the natural law. They summarize and proclaim God's Law. They reveal God's will, and so they bind all people. Jesus taught their true inner spirit.

EXPLORING OUR CATHOLIC FAITH

1. Listening to God's Word

In Colossians 3–4 Paul writes about the ideal Christian life. Read these two chapters of Colossians. In your own words summarize how Paul's teachings address Christians today.

2. Understanding the Teachings of the Catholic Church

The Catholic Church teaches that God calls and helps everyone to live a life of holiness. In your own words, explain what that teaching means.

3. Reflecting on Our Catholic Faith

Saint Augustine of Hippo (A.D. 354–430) shares this insight into our faith: "God is more anxious to bestow His blessings on us than we are to receive them."

4. Living Our Catholic Faith

Living a moral life is spiritual worship. Brainstorm with your group how the precepts of the Church help you live a life of "spiritual worship."

CHAPTER 5

First Three Commandments: Loving God Above All

"You shall love the Lord your God with all your heart,
with all your soul, with all your mind,
and with all your strength."

MARK 12:30

Think about the first three commandments. Brainstorm ways these can be lived. List your ideas here.

What effect does living these commandments have on your life? On society?

A passerby once approached some workers at a building site in medieval France. He asked the first worker, "What are you doing?"

The man sarcastically replied, "Can't you see? I'm trying to cut these marble blocks with these totally useless tools. I'm bored to death, sweating my brains out on this useless job."

The visitor left in a hurry and approached a second worker and put the same question to him. The laborer answered, "Can't you see? I am building a cathedral for God."

Some people ridicule the Ten Commandments as "boring tools." What is your opinion? What kind of person does living by the Ten Commandments build? What kind of society?

KEY TERMS

apostasy

atheism

blasphemy

despair

heresy

idolatry

perjury

sacrilege

schism

superstition

The members of the Society of Jesus, the Jesuits, derive a great motto from their founder Saint Ignatius of Loyola: *Ad Majorem Dei Gloriam*—AMDG—which means, "For the greater glory of God." When we dedicate our work to glorify God, the ordinary becomes extraordinary, as it did for the second worker in the opening story. In this chapter we will be looking at the first three commandments, which highlight our duties toward God—simply because he is God, our Father and Lord.

(*Catechism of the Catholic Church*, 2083–2141)

The First Commandment

God has created us and endowed us with gifts and talents. He has also restored us to his friendship through his Son, Jesus Christ, destining us for eternal glory. Living the first commandment expresses our adoration and praise of God, simply because he is God, and our gratitude to God for all he has given us. The first commandment teaches:

> I am the LORD your God: you shall not have strange gods before me.

Faith, Hope, and Love

The theological virtues of faith, hope, and charity (love) help us honor our loving God. Faith is our first duty to God. It helps us believe in, worship, and witness to God. Hope enables us to trust in God's mercy, God's Word, and God's promise of eternal life. Hope also helps us avoid offending God, which can lead to eternal punishment. Finally, charity empowers us to love God above everything and to love God's creatures because of and for him.

The Virtue of Religion

Faith, hope, and charity animate the moral virtues, especially justice, which enables us to give God what is his due. The virtue of religion makes it possible for us to know and to love God. The word *religion* comes from the Latin word meaning "to bind together." The virtue of religion binds us to God, the source of life and all that is good, who invites us to share in his very own divine life and love. The virtue of religion expresses itself in **adoration,** prayer, sacrifice, and fidelity to one's promises and vows.

Adoration. Adoration acknowledges that God is the Creator and Master of all that exists. When we adore God, we recognize that God is God and we are not. Without God, we are nothing. Humility enables us to turn our lives over to God in praise and thanksgiving for all he has done for us.

Prayer. Prayer lifts our minds and hearts to God. It takes many forms: praise, sorrow, thanksgiving, petition, intercession. Prayer is a powerful help to gain God's strength so we can follow his commandments.

Sacrifice. Sacrifice is a sign of adoration and gratitude. *Sacrifice* means "to make holy." When sacrifice is genuine, it comes from within—from hearts given totally to God. Our lives are most pleasing to God when we join them to the only perfect sacrifice, that of Jesus Christ, who poured out his life for us on a cross. For Catholics, participating in the Eucharist is the preeminent way to worship and pray to God. It joins us to the sacrifice of Jesus Christ, who makes us holy.

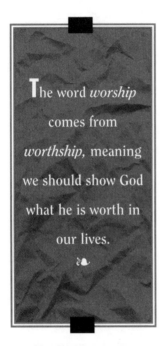

The word *worship* comes from *worthship*, meaning we should show God what he is worth in our lives.

Promises and vows. When we keep our promises to God, for example, the promises that we make in Confirmation or Matrimony, we are practicing an important dimension of our religion.

Vows are free promises made to God for a possible or better good. Some vows are made by devoted people who dedicate themselves to God by promising to do some special work. Men and women in religious communities recognized by the Church vow or promise to live the evangelical counsels of poverty, chastity, and obedience.

Freedom of Religion

For both individuals and communities, the freedom to worship God is a basic human right. Civil laws must protect it. People should not be forced to act against their religious convictions or be stopped from conscientious religious practice, within due limits. Religious expression must be free because love itself is free or it is not love.

People are searching for the truth and for the good. Catholics have a duty to help people discover what is true and good. We do so when we proclaim in word and deed the truth of the Gospel of Jesus and his Church. As a community of faith, we recognize that we are specially blessed to be part of Christ's Body. This is why we must share the truth of our faith with others. However, we must do so respectfully with love, patience, and prudence.

.... Discuss: The Constitution of the United States of America guarantees freedom of religion. In your opinion, in what ways does that free a person to practice religion?

In what ways might it hinder or be an obstacle to the free practice of religion?

Listening to the Word of God

The psalms beautifully express the religious sentiments felt by believers throughout the ages. By reading and praying the psalms, we express our worship and honor and love of God. Read and reflect on these psalms. Respond to the reflection questions in the space provided.

Psalm 5: Cry for Help
Why does the psalmist feel he can approach God for worship?

Psalm 16: Praise
Write out your favorite verse from this psalm.

Psalm 49: Trust in God
What can one's riches never buy (verses 7–10)?

Psalm 51: Repentance
Write out the verse that best expresses for you the cry of repentance.

Psalm 92: Thanksgiving
Name one thing for which the psalmist is thankful.

Offenses against the Virtues of Faith, Hope, and Love

Many attitudes, acts, and failures to act work against living our call to love God above everything. These include sins against faith, hope, and charity, the theological virtues that bind us to God.

Sins against faith. People commit sins against faith when they refuse to accept the truth of something God has revealed or the Church holds out for belief. Incredulity neglects revealed truth or willfully refuses to believe it. **Heresy** denies some truth that is central to our Catholic faith. **Apostasy** totally repudiates Christ and the Christian faith. And **schism** is a refusal to submit to the teaching authority of the pope or to stay in union with those Christians subject to him.

Sins against hope. Presumption and despair are serious failures in the practice of Christian hope. Presumption holds that people can save themselves without God's help. Or it claims that God will save us without any effort on our part to repent of our sins or cooperate with God's grace. People who **despair** abandon all hope that God will save them, forgive their sins, or bestow his redemptive graces on them. Despair abandons hope and trust in God, who is rich in mercy and forever faithful to his promises.

Sins against charity. Sins against charity include religious indifference, neglecting or refusing God's love, ingratitude, spiritual laziness, and outright hatred of God. The source of hatred is pride. It seriously offends an all-good God of abundant love.

Violations of the First Commandment

When Satan tempted Jesus, he rejected the devil by saying, "It is written:

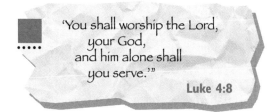

'You shall worship the Lord, your God, and him alone shall you serve.'"

Luke 4:8

Some practices are contrary to true worship and humble service of our loving God. These include such sins as superstition, idolatry, divination, magic, irreligion, atheism, and agnosticism.

❏ **Superstition** attributes magical powers to certain objects, acts, words, or religious practices apart from interior religious attitudes like faith and humility.

❏ **Idolatry** often takes the form of worshiping many gods (polytheism). In today's world, it also takes the form of making sex, pleasure, power, money, the state, and the like, our god. Worshiping a "good" by making it our "god" turns us away from our relationship with the loving God, who is the source of all goods.

❏ Divination tries to discover what is hidden (occult). It also attempts to look into the future. Divination will resort to calling on Satan or other devils, conjuring up dead spirits, and practicing astrology or reading horoscopes. It also involves palm reading and playing with Ouija boards. These types of actions disrespect a provident God, who wants us to trust his loving care over our lives and our futures.

- Magic or sorcery attempts to "tame occult powers, so as to place them at one's service and have a supernatural power over others" (CCC, 2117).

- Irreligion includes the sins of tempting God in words and deeds; sacrilege, and simony. We "tempt" God by daring God to show forth his goodness or wisdom. The Church has always taught that this type of challenge profoundly disrespects God and shows a lack of trust in a loving, provident Creator.

  Sacrilege is the "profaning or treating unworthily the sacraments and other liturgical actions, as well as persons, things, or places consecrated to God" (CCC, 2120). Sacrilege is a grave sin, most especially when directed against the eucharistic Christ.

  Simony is the buying or selling of spiritual graces. We cannot buy God's graces. They are free gifts. We can only receive them with grateful hearts.

- **Atheism** is a grave rejection or denial of the existence of God. Various forms of atheism exist in our world today. For example, materialists claim only realities that can be sensed are real. For materialists there are no spiritual realities, neither God nor a human soul. Atheistic humanism makes a god out of humanity, the sole maker and controller of its own destiny. They have no room for God. Contemporary atheism focuses on economic and social theories as the ultimate source of human freedom. "Atheism is often based on a false conception of human autonomy, exaggerated to

Venerating Sacred Images

The veneration of sacred images is not contrary to the first commandment. Since God became human in Jesus Christ, it is most fitting for Christians to use icons, pictures, mosaics, and statues of Jesus, the Blessed Mother, the angels, and the saints. These sacred images call to mind these holy people and point us to them.

We do not *worship* these images, as it is forbidden by God's command: "Be strictly on your guard, therefore, not to degrade yourselves by fashioning an idol" (Deuteronomy 4:15–16). We worship God alone. Sacred images merely serve to remind us of God's love for us.

List the sacred images that help you focus your life on God.

In what ways do they help you worship God?

the point of refusing any dependence on God" (CCC, 2126; see *Pastoral Constitution on the Church in the Modern World*, 20 § 1). Christians know that our human dignity is fully realized only when we acknowledge truth, the existence of a loving Creator, and turn our lives over to God.

❑ Agnosticism denies that it is possible to know with certainty that God exists. Therefore, agnostics are indifferent to the question. They decide not to decide. In effect, many agnostics are *practical atheists* who live their lives as though there were no God.

(CCC, 2142–2167)

The Second Commandment

Scripture teaches us that the name of a person and the person himself or herself are inseparable. This helps us understand the heart of the second commandment, which teaches us:

> You shall not take the name of the LORD, your God, in vain.

Values Taught by the Second Commandment

"Among all the words of Revelation, there is one which is unique: the revealed name of God. God confides his name to those who believe in him; he reveals himself to them in his personal mystery. The gift of a name belongs to the order of trust and intimacy. 'The Lord's name is holy' " (CCC, 2143).

Respect for the name of God. Respect for God's name is an expression of the respect for God. We show great reverence for God's name when we witness to our faith in one, true, holy God and venerate the name of Jesus, of Mary, and of the saints. When we sign ourselves "in the name of the Father and of the Son and of the Holy Spirit," we proclaim our faith in the Triune God who made, saves, and sanctifies us.

When we pray at the start of our day or before beginning any activity with the Sign of the Cross, we acknowledge God's presence with us. Praying the Sign of the Cross will remind us to whom we belong—the only Person worthy of our total dedication, respect, and praise.

Respect for each other's name. We were baptized into the Christian community "in the name of the Father, and the Son, and the Holy Spirit" and received our name in the church community. God calls each one by name (see Isaiah 43:1, John 10:3). Whatever our name, everyone's name is sacred. "The name is the icon of the person. It demands respect as a sign of the dignity of the one who bears it" (CCC, 2158).

Actions Contrary to the Second Commandment

The second commandment calls us to give witness to our faith in God by the way we speak of God and the sacred. Certain actions are clear signs that we are not living the second commandment. For example:

❑ The abuse of the name of God, the Son of God, Jesus Christ, Mary, or any of the saints is wrong.

❑ We are unfaithful to God when we break promises made in God's name.

- **Blasphemy** is any thought, word, or act that expresses hate, contempt, or defiance against God and Jesus Christ. It is gravely and intrinsically evil and can *never* be justified. We can also blaspheme against the Church, the saints, or holy things. To invoke God's name to enslave, torture, or kill people or to evade a crime is also blasphemous.

- **Perjury** is lying under oath. False oaths call on God to witness to a lie. People who perjure themselves deliberately deceive others by taking an oath while intending not to keep it. The taking of an oath with the intent to commit wrongdoing is a serious evil that dishonors God. It is a grave offense against the Lord, who is always faithful to his promises.

Catholic tradition, following Saint Paul, allows us to take oaths for serious and morally correct reasons, for example, in a legal trial. However, we may never take oaths to evil governments or legal bodies that attack human dignity or fracture Christian unity.

Swearing is taking an oath by calling upon God under oath to witness to the truthfulness of our statements. Calling upon God, who is truth, in this way must always conform to the truth. Failing to do so is using God's name in vain. In the Sermon on the Mount, Jesus teaches us followers to live always in the truth. Our "yes" should mean "yes." Our "no" should mean "no" (see Matthew 5:37).

Breaking an oath that we make when calling upon God as our witness is seriously wrong. It "witnesses" to our disrespect for God.

What the Documents Say

The bishops of the Church gathered at the Second Vatican Council taught about the importance for us to worship God in community. They taught:

> [The] social nature [of man] requires that man give external expression to these internal acts of religion, that he communicate with others on religious matters, and profess his religion in community.
>
> *Declaration on Religious Liberty*, 3

How does this passage help you understand the Church's teaching about participation in Mass on Sunday and holy days of obligation?

The Third Commandment

Scripture tells us that on the seventh day of creation, God rested. By establishing the sabbath rest, God gave us a model. Jews and Christians alike have declared the sabbath to be a day of rest. The Sabbath, which represented the completion of the first creation, has been replaced for Christians by Sunday, which recalls the new creation inaugurated by the Resurrection of the Lord. The third commandment is: Remember to keep holy the LORD's Day.

The Values Taught by the Third Commandment

The third commandment reminds us of God's creative activity on the first six days of the week and of his rest on the seventh, or the Sabbath day. It also memorializes God's covenant with the Israelites, whom he freed from slavery in Egypt and gave the Sabbath as a sign of his irrevocable covenant of love.

The Sabbath. On the Sabbath, the Israelites were to praise God, God's creation, and his saving acts. We should make this day a day of refreshment and break from ordinary work. We are to remember our dependence on God and to worship and thank him. We are to renew our bodies and spirits.

Jesus always respected the holiness of the Sabbath, though his enemies often accused him of violating the sabbath law. He taught, "The sabbath was made for man, not man for the sabbath" (Mark 2:27).

The Lord's Day. While the Jewish people celebrate the Sabbath on Saturday, Christians celebrate the day of Christ's resurrection on the "eighth day," Sunday, which is called the Lord's Day. On it we commemorate the Paschal mystery of his passion, death, resurrection, and glorification.

We come together on this holy day to recall his passover from death to eternal life, an event that won for us salvation. We praise, worship, and thank the Father for the gift of the Son and all the blessings he and the Holy Spirit shower on us.

From the apostolic age, Christians have kept the sabbath law by worshiping God, assembling for the Eucharist in memory of Jesus as he asked us to do at the Last Supper. Sunday is the Christian holy day, a commemoration of God's decisive act of love for us through Jesus Christ.

Do I Have to Go to Mass on Sundays?

Simply, the answer is yes! Church law requires Catholics to participate at the celebration of Mass on Saturday evening or on Sunday and all other holy days of obligation.

Why? Because the Eucharist is the very heart and foundation of Catholic life. It proclaims and celebrates all that God has done for us, especially in Jesus Christ. By participating in Mass, we are testifying to the world that we belong to Jesus Christ and that we are vital members of his Body, the Church.

Those who come to celebrate who they are and receive the Lord in Holy Communion are making a powerful statement. They are saying they are the Body of Christ; they are one with Christ and with one another. They are thanking God (eucharist means "thanksgiving") for their life, health, friends, families, love—for everything, especially for the gift of the Lord Jesus Christ.

Someone wryly remarked that everyone can come up with a reason for not going to Mass—even those who do come. What reasons do people give for not going to Mass? How do these reasons "measure up" against the teaching of the Church on why going to Mass is such a serious duty and responsibility?

Sunday is to be observed as the foremost holy day of obligation in the universal Church. Led by our pastors, Catholics today gather in parish communities to express, celebrate, and deepen our unity in Christ Jesus. When we do, we are doing what he asked. We receive the Lord in Holy Communion. This great gift empowers us to live holy, moral, and Christian lives both individually and as his community, the Body of Christ, in our world today.

Keeping Sunday Holy

The third commandment requires that we make the Lord's Day holy. On Sundays and other holy days of obligation, we are bound to participate in Mass, and to abstain from those labors and business concerns that impede the worship to be rendered to God, the joy that is proper to the Lord's Day, or the proper relaxation of mind and body.

We do so by relaxing, spending time with our families, and doing acts of service for the poor, needy, and elderly. Other "sanctifying" activities of rest and refreshment include reading, reflecting, meditating, and enjoying the beauty of God's natural world. Still others include cultural activities that refresh our spirits, hearts, and minds. Participating in these activities helps us develop our family, cultural, social, and religious lives. Every Christian should avoid making unnecessary demands on others that would hinder them from observing the Lord's Day.

Some people have necessary work to do on Sundays. They should set aside time for prayer, reflection, and rest. We must take care not to make unnecessary demands that would prevent others from enjoying their sabbath rest.

A Day of Worship, Rest, and Re-creation

Observance of the Lord's Day gives us the chance to nurture aspects of our lives necessary for a full and happy life. These include family, cultural, social, and religious pursuits. (See CCC, 2184.)

Here are some practices mentioned by the *Catechism* that help us keep holy the Lord's Day. Check the appropriate column that reflects your typical Sunday.

1 = I always do this.   3 = I rarely do this.
2 = I often do this.   4 = I never do this.

The Practice

1. I go to Sunday or Saturday evening Mass to worship and thank God and to receive the Lord in Holy Communion.   **1   2   3   4**

2. I refrain from unnecessary shopping on Sundays.   **1   2   3   4**

3. I spend quality time with my family.   **1   2   3   4**

4. I engage in some work of service with the sick, infirm, or elderly. For example, I might visit my grandparents.   **1   2   3   4**

5. I take time to pray and reflect on my Christian life.   **1   2   3   4**

6. I listen to quality music or engage in some other cultural pursuit like seeing an uplifting movie or going to a museum.   **1   2   3   4**

7. I read something that stretches my mind or elevates my spirit.   **1   2   3   4**

8. I enjoy the beauty of God's creation by spending time outside enjoying nature.   **1   2   3   4**

9. I play a sport that helps me unwind.   **1   2   3   4**

10. Write your own here: _____   **1   2   3   4**

Brainstorm: List some Sunday activities that would be good ways for young people to observe the law of sabbath rest.

Prayer

Thanking, praising, and glorifying God—simply because he is God—is a basic element of Christian prayer. When we praise and thank God, we are acknowledging more the Giver than the gifts he has given to us. The first three commandments instruct us to do just that. The New Testament is a great help in showing us how. Pray the following prayer of thanks to the Father for our new life in Christ Jesus.

We thank and glorify you,

Father,

for setting us apart,

for uniting us to Christ Jesus,

for placing his mark

of ownership on us,

for giving us the Holy Spirit

in our hearts,

the Spirit who guarantees

all that you have in store for us.

Amen.

Based on 2 Corinthians 1:20–22

REVIEW

IMPORTANT TERMS TO KNOW

apostasy—the total rejection of Christ and the Christian faith by a baptized Christian

atheism—the denial of God's existence

blasphemy—any thought, word, or act that expresses hatred or contempt for God; the use of the name of God, of Jesus Christ, of the Virgin Mary, of the saints, of the Church, or of holy things in an offensive way

despair—the abandoning of all hope in God's saving graces or any hope of salvation

heresy—the deliberate and stubborn denial of a central teaching of the Catholic faith

idolatry—the worshiping of something other than the true God

perjury—lying under oath, calling on God to witness to a lie

sacrilege—contemptuous treatment of a holy person, place, action, or thing specially dedicated to God

schism—a break in Christian unity caused by a refusal to submit to the authority of the pope or remain united to those Christians who are subject to him

superstition—the deviation of religious feeling and the practices this feeling imposes

CHAPTER SUMMARY

1. The first commandment calls us to believe in God, to hope in him, and to love him above all else. The theological virtues of faith, hope, and love help us honor our loving God.

2. The virtue of religion enables us to know and to love God. It expresses itself in adoration, prayer, sacrifice, and fidelity to our vows and promises.

3. Heresy, apostasy, schism, presumption, despair, religious indifference, ingratitude, and outright hatred of God are offenses against the first commandment.

4. Superstition, idolatry, divination, magic, irreligion, atheism, and agnosticism violate the true worship we owe God.

5. The second commandment requires that we reverence the name of God. We must

also reverence the name of Jesus Christ, of the Virgin Mary, and the saints.

6. The second commandment forbids every improper use of God's name. Blasphemy, oath-breaking, perjury, and cursing are contrary to this commandment.

7. The third commandment requires that we keep the Lord's Day holy. The Sabbath, which represented the completion of the first creation, has been replaced for Christians by Sunday, which recalls the new creation inaugurated by the Resurrection.

8. On Sundays and other holy days of obligation the faithful are bound to abstain from those labors and business concerns that impede the worship to be rendered to God, the joy that is proper to the Lord's Day, or the proper relaxation of mind and body.

EXPLORING OUR CATHOLIC FAITH

1. Listening to God's Word

The Letter to James clearly teaches us about the power of human speech—and our responsibility to use that gift. Read and reflect on James 3:7–10. Think about the words of James and think about your own use of your gift of speech. Why is it that so many consider the use of offensive or vulgar language a sign of maturity?

2. Understanding the Teachings of the Catholic Church

The bishops at the Second Vatican Council observed that believers, because of the way they are not living as followers of Christ "have more than a little to do with the rise of atheism" (*Pastoral Constitution on the Church in the*

Modern World, 19). What do you think the bishops are saying?

3. Reflecting on Our Catholic Faith

Reflect on this insight into our relationship with God: "God without humans is still God; humans without God are nothing." How does that insight help you appreciate your value? How does it help you evaluate your relationship with others? Your use of material goods? Write your reflections in your journal.

4. Living Our Catholic Faith

Prayer is conversing with God. Talking and listening are two important parts of any conversation. Try a ten-minute conversation with God each day for the next week.

CHAPTER 6

The Fourth Commandment: Loving the Family

With your whole heart honor your father;
your mother's birthpangs forget not.
Remember, of these parents you were born;
what can you give them for all they gave you?
SIRACH 7:27–28

Explain why you agree or disagree with these statements.

1. A child must do everything a parent asks.

2. The state must guarantee parents the right to choose for their children a school that corresponds to their convictions.

3. We have a moral duty to pay taxes.

A college freshman wrote this letter to his parents. He had not written in three months:

Dear Mom and Dad,

Hope everyone at home is okay. I really apologize for not writing for so long, but I didn't want you to worry about the fire in my dorm and the week stay I had in the local hospital for smoke inhalation. It was really not that bad for me because I met a student nurse there who is really attractive. She and I really like each other a lot; in fact, I moved in with her to share a spare room she has in her off-campus apartment. I want you to know we are deeply in love and that you'll both be grandparents sooner than you ever expected.

In conclusion, give me a call sometime soon. I hope you'll stop worrying about me. There was no dorm fire; I wasn't in the hospital and, sad to say, I don't have a girlfriend. I told you all this because I am getting a "D" in biology and probably will have to drop out of premed. I just wanted to put things in perspective.

I love you guys a lot.

What do you think about the tactics of the college student?

Interestingly, the fourth commandment, which deals with honoring one's parents, is the first commandment listed in the second tablet of the Decalogue. This signifies the centrality of loving our parents and our families who have given us life. In this chapter we will look at what it means to honor our parents and to live as loving members of our family. It will also review our obligations to honor and respect all those in the other communities in which we live whom God has invested with authority to lead and govern those communities.

(*Catechism of the Catholic Church,* 2196–2213)

Honor, Respect, Obedience

The fourth commandment is: Honor your father and your mother. This commandment promotes the values of **honor** and **respect,** affection and gratitude, and **obedience.** It first speaks to the relationship between children and their parents, which is the foundational relationship we have.

This commandment, however, also concerns kinship ties we have with our extended family. It treats the duties and responsibilities that exist between pupils and teachers, employers and employees, citizens and civic authorities.

Honoring Parents

The very wording of the fourth commandment states its reward: "Honor your father and your mother, that you may have a long life in the land which the Lord, your God, is giving you" (Exodus 20:12). Peace and harmony will come about if we strive to live the values underlying this commandment. On the other hand, if we neglect God's command to honor our parents, great harm will befall both individuals and the human community.

Honor is the key value underlying the fourth commandment. It is closely tied to love and flows from the virtue of justice. For the writers of the Bible, a situation is *just* when everything is in right relationship— when things are as God created them to be. When we honor someone, we acknowledge the other person to be someone whom we love and respect.

The relationship binding parent and child is a foundational relationship— more important than any other relationship between humans. Not only are children to honor their parents and those in authority over them, but parents, teachers, employers, and other authority figures must also honor and respect those who are in their care. Mutual honor puts love and justice into practice. Living the fourth commandment results in harmonious living that helps members of families and other communities live peacefully.

What the Documents Say

The bishops of the Church gathered at the Second Vatican Council taught:

> The mission of being the primary vital cell of society has been given to the family by God himself. This mission will be accomplished if the family, by the mutual affection of its members and by family prayer, presents itself as a domestic sanctuary of the Church; if the whole family takes its part in the Church's liturgical worship; if, finally, it offers active hospitality, and practises justice and other good works for the benefit of all . . . suffering from want.
>
> *Decree on the Apostolate of Lay People,* 11

What are the basic responsibilities a Christian family has to fulfill its mission to be the first and vital cell of society?

In what ways do you see Catholic families meeting these responsibilities?

The Family in God's Plan

The **family** is the foundational community of human life. It exists for the good of the wife and husband and for the procreation and education of children. (See Ephesians 5:31–32.)

Children and parents have equal dignity and share in a variety of responsibilities, rights, and duties. The closer we build family life on the values of this commandment, the stronger individual families and other larger societies, including the Christian community, will be.

The family teaches us how to be human and live as children of God. The family sheds light on all of our relationships in society. In the family, we learn how to respect others and how to value them as persons, children of God who are worthy of our respect and attention. We learn how and why to care for the young and the elderly, the sick and disabled and the poor. We learn how and why to respect, love, and care for members of our extended families, our fellow citizens, and all members of the human community.

The Domestic Church

We learn to love in the family, especially in the *Christian* family, which we call the **domestic church.** The Christian family is a wonderful communion of persons that images the Holy Trinity—the communion of the Father and the Son united in the Holy Spirit. In the domestic church, the community of faith, hope, and love, we learn as children to pray and listen to God's Word. In the Christian family, we learn love and respect—virtues necessary for the prosperity of all the communities to which we belong.

Governments and the Family

Civil authorities have a serious obligation and responsibility to support family life and married life. They do this by creating laws and other civic institutions that guarantee the basic human rights families need to prosper and live in harmony. These include such fundamental rights as:

❏ the right to private property, decent housing, and employment;

❏ the right of individuals to marry and have children and to profess and hand on their religious faith to their offspring;
❏ the right to health care;
❏ the right to a safe and healthy environment that protects families from such evils as illegal drugs and pornography;
❏ the right to associate freely with other families to obtain adequate representation in the political order.

Read and reflect on these Scripture passages. In the spaces provided summarize the key message of each passage.

Proverbs 1:8–9

Proverbs 20:11

Deuteronomy 6:5–7

Hebrews 12:11

Colossians 3:12–15

List five qualities mentioned in these passages that would help families live in harmony. Discuss the reasons for your choices.

1. _____

2. _____

3. _____

4 _____

5. _____

Duties and Responsibilities

Reflecting on the fourth commandment, the Church teaches that there are certain duties and responsibilities that flow from this command of the Decalogue.

The Duties of Children

Respect, honor, and gratitude are the foundation of the relationship between parents and children. Our respect for our parents flows from their giving us the gift of life. This respect includes a willingness to be guided by our parents as our first teachers.

Parents receive their **authority** from God to help and guide their children. Honor calls for the "just" obeying of our parents when they ask us to do what is good for us or for our family. When we obey our parents, we are acknowledging God, the source of all life and authority.

Honoring and respecting our parents does not stop after we reach adulthood. As adult children we honor and respect our parents by continuing to seek their advice and learn from their experience. We show our gratitude to our aged parents by supporting them financially, psychologically, and spiritually in times of sickness, distress, and loneliness.

Respect is also the foundation of the relationship between brothers and sisters. Fair play, honesty, patience, sacrifice, and love toward siblings contribute immensely toward making a family a caring community.

Must I obey my parents in all things?

In general, the answer is yes. Scripture and the Tradition of the Church command it. (See Ephesians 6:1, 4.)

Children honor their parents through obedience; parents honor their children through good example and loving instruction. There is one exception: Children must not obey an immoral command given by their parents or any other authority figure. Following God's Law supersedes obedience to any earthly authority.

Discuss: Why are honor, respect, and obedience at the heart of family life?

We are also to respect, honor, and show our gratitude to those who have shared the gifts of faith, baptism, and the Christian life with us. In addition to parents, grandparents, and other family members, these people include priests, religion teachers, and other friends and teachers. A wonderful way to show our thanks is to live the Christian life that our spiritual mentors have taught us.

The Duties of Parents

The fundamental duty and responsibility of parents is to "regard their children as *children of God* and respect them as *human persons*. Showing themselves obedient to the will of the Father in heaven, they educate their children to fulfill God's law" (CCC, 2222). This education includes not only the intellectual education of children, but also their moral education and spiritual formation as well.

Parents have the privilege and duty of handing on the Christian faith to their children. Our parents are our primary teachers, bringing us up "to keep God's commandments as Christ taught us, by loving God and our neighbor" (*Rite of Baptism for Children*, 77). To help them fulfill this responsibility our parents have a basic and inalienable right to choose schools that correspond to their own deeply held convictions.

Protecting their family from the degrading influences in society and media is a particularly important responsibility in today's world.

Parents exercise this responsibility in many ways. They give good example to their children, treating them as special children of God who deserve profound respect. They help their children discover how special they are in God's eyes. They do their best to create a home in which children experience love, warmth, caring, tenderness, forgiveness, and self-sacrificing service. If they admit their shortcomings, they will more authentically—and responsibly—guide their children's growth.

Finally, the duties and responsibilities of parents include respecting their grown children's right and duty to choose their own profession and state in life. Parents should joyfully support children whom God calls to serve him as a professed religious or in the ordained ministry.

The Christian family's primary function is to lead its members to Jesus Christ, who is "the way and the truth and the life (John 14:6)." Following the Lord means belonging to God's family, where the kinship ties are not blood but our relationship with Christy. The good example of parents' wholehearted participation in the Eucharist and parish life will help children grow in faith and holiness.

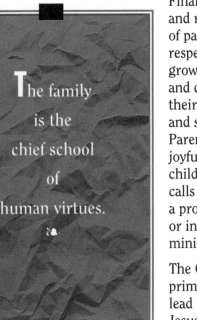

The family is the chief school of human virtues.

Parents and You

Pope John Paul II writes:

"To honor" means to acknowledge! We could put it this way: "Let yourself be guided by the firm acknowledgment of the person, first of all that of your father and mother, and then that of the other members of the family." Honor is essentially an attitude of unselfishness . . . If the Fourth Commandment demands that honor should be shown to our father and mother, it also makes this demand out of concern for the good of the family.

Letter to Families for the International Year of the Family, 15

List five ways you honor *your* parents.

Respond to the following questions—honestly and honorably.

Acknowledgment: What do you acknowledge to be the three best qualities of your parents?

Unselfish cooperation: Examine your relationship with your parents. Circle the appropriate number: 1 = excellent; 5 = needs lots of improvement.

1. I acknowledge their authority as coming from God. **1 2 3 4 5**

2. I express my gratitude for all they have done and are doing for me. **1 2 3 4 5**

3. I unselfishly respond to the needs of other family members. **1 2 3 4 5**

Communication: How well do you know your parents? Briefly answer what you think they would say about these moral issues.

1. Cheating on tests

2. Premarital sexual intercourse

3. Prejudicial jokes

4. Abortion

5. Alcohol use by teens

Share your responses with your parents.

The Duties of Civil Authorities and Citizens

The fourth commandment also guides civil authorities and citizens. All authority in a society is a sacred trust from God, the source of all authority, and is in service to the good of all citizens. Those in positions of authority must protect and defend fundamental human and political rights. They must never order anyone to do anything contrary to human dignity or the natural law. Civil authorities have the responsibility to treat all citizens equitably, keeping in mind the needs and contributions of each member of society.

On the other hand, as citizens we should respect those who have the responsibility to lead and govern our communities. We should help civil authorities by contributing to the common good in truth, solidarity, freedom, and justice. This is why we as citizens have a moral obligation to pay taxes, vote, and defend our country. Moreover, those of us who are citizens of wealthier and more developed nations are to warmly welcome immigrants who are searching for a safe country in which to work and live.

Those of us blessed with Christian faith have an added responsibility. We must always speak the truth in love to our fellow citizens. We are called to help human institutions organize in light of the Gospel. All too often societies turn to forms of government or write laws that violate human rights. While the Catholic Church respects and supports political freedom and responsible citizenship, we have the responsibility to speak out on moral issues that threaten human rights or endanger people's salvation.

The Gospel in My Life

Recall the teaching of Jesus in which he tells us we are to fulfill our duties as citizens, but when civil authority commands something contrary to human dignity, the natural law, or a gospel teaching, we *must* refuse to obey it. (See Matthew 22:21.)

Brainstorm examples of civil laws that you think are against God's law.

Discuss: God's Law supersedes civil law.

Prayer

We are children of God. We need God's help to live a Christian moral life. We call God "Abba," a loving Father who loves us beyond compare and who answers our requests by giving us what we need rather than what we want. A prayer-poem by an anonymous author puts it well. Reflect on its many truths.

> I prayed for strength
>   that I might achieve;
> I was made weak
>   that I might obey.
> I prayed for health
>   that I might do great things;
> I was given infirmity
>   that I might do better things.
> I prayed for riches
>   that I might be happy;
> I was given poverty
>   that I might be wise.
> I prayed for power
>   that I might have the praise
>   of men;
> I was given weakness
>   that I might feel the need of
>   God.
> I prayed for all things
>   that I might enjoy life;
> I was given life
>   that I might enjoy all things.
> I received nothing that I asked
>   for—all that I hoped for;
> My prayers were answered—
>   I am most blessed.

REVIEW

IMPORTANT TERMS TO KNOW

authority—the God-given responsibility to guide others in living and growing in the life given to them by God

domestic church—name given to the Christian family, a community of faith, hope, and charity—a sign of the Holy Trinity

family—the original cell of all social life, in which a husband and wife commit themselves to share the gift of love and life

honor—respect shown to someone because of their dignity as a child of God or their relationship and responsibility of authority in our regard

obedience—the submission of our conduct to those in true authority over us; this submission to parents, civil authorities, and so on, is conditional upon the moral rightness of what they ask us to do

respect—familial piety, which calls for faithfulness in our relationships with parents and other family members

CHAPTER SUMMARY

When Christian families—parents and children alike—and civic leaders and citizens live by the values of the fourth commandment, peace and harmony will result. In this chapter we learned:

1. The fourth commandment promotes the values of honor and respect, affection and gratitude, and obedience. We honor others when we acknowledge them as gifts to respect and to love.

2. The family is the original unit of social life. It is the school for learning love and all the virtues.

3. The Christian family is the domestic church. It is a communion of persons living in faith, hope, and love; it is an image of the communion that is the Holy Trinity.

4. Children have a serious duty to express gratitude to their parents for the gift of life. They do so when they respect, honor, and obey their parents.

5. Parents have the fundamental duty and right to educate their children. They do so by treating children with mutual respect, and providing good example, forgiving hearts, and wise counsel.

6. Authority in society is a sacred trust from God, who is the source of all authority. Governments must support the family and the institution of marriage.

7. Citizens should honor, respect, and obey all legitimate authority as God's representatives. Citizens have a duty to contribute to the common good.

8. Neither children nor citizens should obey directives from parents or others in authority that are contrary to human dignity, the natural law, or gospel teaching.

EXPLORING OUR CATHOLIC FAITH

1. Listening to God's Word

The Book of Sirach belongs to the wisdom literature of the Old Testament. Read and reflect on Sirach 7:27–28. Think about Sirach's closing question. How would you respond?

2. Understanding the Teachings of the Catholic Church

The Catholic Church teaches that adult children continue to have responsibilities toward their elderly parents. What does that teaching mean? How important is it in our times when people are living longer lives?

3. Reflecting on Our Catholic Faith

Saint Irenaeus (c. A.D. 140–c. A.D. 202) taught that it is through obedience and discipline and training that we grow into the image and likeness of God. In what ways does this insight help you live the fourth commandment? Write your reflections in your journal.

4. Living Our Catholic Faith

The Christian family is the domestic church. Brainstorm with several other members of your group a list of rules that would help a Christian family live its vocation as domestic church.

CHAPTER 7

The Fifth Commandment: Love and Respect Life

In this hand is the soul of every living thing,
and the life breath of all mankind.

JOB 12:10

A story about the great Leonardo da Vinci recounts that he had a violent argument with another artist right before painting his famous *Last Supper*. So full of emotion was Leonardo, that he depicted Judas's face with that of his artist enemy.

However, when da Vinci tried to paint the face of Jesus, he could not do so. No matter how hard he tried, he failed at every attempt. After thinking and praying about it, da Vinci concluded that he could not paint Jesus' face because he painted his enemy's face on Judas. So the great artist painted over the face of Judas. He once again began painting the face of Jesus—this time successfully.

KEY TERMS

abortion

arms race

euthanasia

murder

scandal

suicide

How might the feelings of revenge affect a person's decisions? A person's actions?

Leonardo da Vinci learned an important lesson. It is impossible to hold an image of the loving Jesus in our heart if we harbor bitterness and resentment toward our enemies. This chapter deals with the fifth commandment, which forbids killing and the hatred and anger that lead us to disrespect God's precious gift of human life.

(Catechism of the Catholic Church, 2258–2267)

The Sacredness of Human Life

Every human life is sacred. From the very first moment of our conception, we are sacred. We have a relationship with the living God who gives us the gift of life and invites us to live in relationship with him forever.

God Is the Author of Life

The fifth commandment simply decrees, "Do not kill." This straightforward prohibition stresses the sacredness of all human life. It forcefully tells us that God alone is the Author of Life and that we are the stewards of life. God entrusts us to cherish and care for this precious gift. Only God is the Lord of life.

The biblical story of Cain's **murder** of his brother Abel teaches that murder, the killing of innocent people, is a consequence of original sin. Murder results from envy and anger and is a grave violation of the commandment to love one's neighbor and an affront to a holy God who created us out of love. The prohibition of murder—the killing of an innocent person—is always binding on all people, in all places, for all times.

God's Word in My Life

Read Genesis 4:1–16, the story of Cain and Abel.
What does Cain say to God that has often been repeated (verse 9)?

In what ways have you seen or heard the story of Cain and Abel played out again and again?

In the Sermon on the Mount, Jesus commands us to obey the fifth commandment. (See Matthew 5:21–22.) He tells us to root out all hatred, anger, and revenge—vices that eat away at a person's heart and when left unchecked lead to murder.

But Jesus' teaching on the fifth commandment goes beyond the prohibition "Do not kill." Jesus asks us not only to hold our anger in check but to turn the other cheek, to forgive and love our enemies. (See Matthew 5:22–39, 44.) He himself showed us the way. He died looking into the hearts of his persecutors, saying, "Father, forgive them, they know not what they do" (Luke 23:34).

Defense of One's Own Life

We are called to respect not only the life of others but our own life too. "Love toward oneself," the Church teaches, "remains a fundamental principle of morality. Therefore it is legitimate to insist on respect for one's own right to life" (CCC, 2264). We have the right to defend ourselves against someone who is attempting to take our life. Self-defense is both a right and a duty.

But may we protect ourselves if it means taking the life of the unjust aggressor? The answer is *yes* if it is the only way to defend our life. Using force that is *necessary* to protect our life is a legitimate form of self-defense even when using that force results in the death of the person attacking us. However, the means of defending ourselves must be limited to whatever is necessary to *stop* the person unjustly attacking us. What we directly intend in using that force is the protection of

our life—and not the death of our attacker. The death of our attacker results from protecting our life.

Similarly, people entrusted with protecting the life of others—for example, parents of children—have the right and duty of defending those entrusted to their care.

Capital Punishment

Capital punishment is on the rise in many of the states in our country. Many feel that it is the only way to deal with the growing number of violent crimes and killings on our streets, in our homes, and in our neighborhoods.

What does the Church teach about capital punishment? The Church teaches that government officials have a right and a duty to defend innocent citizens in the face of serious, unjust aggression. It has traditionally recognized that the state has the right to inflict the death penalty to protect citizens against people guilty of heinous crimes.

In recent decades, conferences of bishops, such as the National Council of Catholic Bishops in the United States, have argued against the use of the death penalty. In their *Statement on Capital Punishment* (1980), the Catholic bishops in the United States pointed out that the death penalty seems to contradict a consistent "respect-for-life ethic." They argued that capital punishment cannot reform the criminal and that there is little evidence to prove that it deters criminals. They also pointed out that there is a pattern of discrimination in the use of the death penalty against

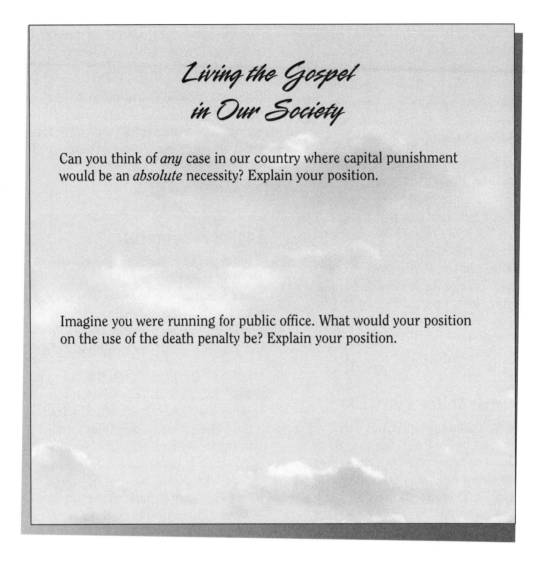

Living the Gospel in Our Society

Can you think of *any* case in our country where capital punishment would be an *absolute* necessity? Explain your position.

Imagine you were running for public office. What would your position on the use of the death penalty be? Explain your position.

people who are poor and cannot afford good legal defense, and members of minority groups in our society.

While the Catholic Church recognizes the right of the state to use the death penalty, it strongly encourages Christian nations not to use such severe punishment—but to demonstrate concretely Christ Jesus' forgiving love. The Church also reminds us that punishment should contribute to the correction of the offender.

Pope John Paul II, in his important encyclical letter *The Gospel of Life,*

taught that because society has many "bloodless" ways to deter crime, governments should use the death penalty *very rarely*. Pope John Paul II teaches that the death penalty is to be used only

> in cases of absolute necessity: in other words, when it would not be possible otherwise to defend society. Today however, as a result of steady improvements in the organization of the penal system, such cases are very rare, if not practically non-existent.
> *The Gospel of Life,* 56

Actions Contrary to the Fifth Commandment

Major violations of God's command to respect life include murder, **abortion, euthanasia,** and **suicide.**

Murder

The fifth commandment forbids the direct and intentional killing of a person. This also includes the prohibition of doing anything with the intention of indirectly bringing about a person's death. Such acts are gravely sinful and can never be justified— even if government authorities order them. The killing of an infant, sibling, parent, or spouse is even more heinous because of the natural bonds with them.

The fifth commandment also forbids us from needlessly exposing others to fatal danger. This command also calls us to come to the aid of another person whose life is in grave danger when we are able to do so. For example, we are to feed people who are hungry when we have the means and opportunity to do so; to fail to come to their aid is not to live up to this commandment. In addition, this command calls us to speak out and name such acts as drunken driving, the selling of illegal drugs, and so on, as serious attacks on the sanctity of human life.

Abortion

The Church unequivocally teaches that all human life "must be respected and protected absolutely from the moment of conception. From the first moment of his existence, a human being must be recognized as having the rights of a person—among which is the inviolable right of every innocent being to life" (CCC, 2270; see CDF, *The Gift of Life,* I, 1).

Protecting the Life of the Embryo. The Catholic Church's teaching on abortion is based on the principle that everyone has a right to life. This right is not conferred by human law. It is a right superior to our right to free choice—and the pursuit of happiness. God has called each of us into existence, and from the very first moment of our conception, our existence, our life is sacred—we are sacred.

The Church clearly teaches that direct abortion, that is, the killing of a nonviolable embryo or fetus as a means or an end, is a serious violation of God's Law. The teaching of the Church has remained unchanged since the first century—and remains unchangeable.

In speaking of abortion, we must clearly distinguish between—and never confuse—the legality of an act and the morality of an act. While some governments have legalized abortion, it remains a grave evil.

A society's laws must protect the fundamental right to life of all its members—born and unborn. This right and the fulfillment of this responsibility of civil authorities is the very backbone of society. Governments that create laws that contradict it undermine the very foundations of society and create a "culture of death" in which no one is safe. Pope John Paul II clearly and strongly taught:

> Nothing and no one can in any way permit the killing of an innocent human being, whether a fetus or an embryo, an infant or an adult, an old person, or one suffering from an incurable disease, or a person who is dying.
>
> *The Gospel of Life,* 57

Caring for the Embryo. Since the embryo from its conception is a developing human person, we are to care for it as we care for all living persons. We can treat it medically, for example, in the case of a prenatal disease. But any procedures that would treat the embryo as disposable matter or lead to abortion are seriously wrong. Genetic manipulations that merely try to produce a baby of a particular sex or one who possesses certain qualities violate the personal dignity of a one-of-a-kind human being created by God. The embryo or fetus "must be defended in its integrity, cared for, and healed, as far as possible, like any other human being" (CCC, 2274).

Abortion is so heinous and immoral that the Church imposes excommunication on any person who has an abortion or cooperates in helping another person abort a fetus. The Church, however, extends Christ's forgiveness to those who repent this grave crime. As Catholics we are to pray for, support, and love those who are contemplating abortion.

Euthanasia

The word *euthanasia* comes from a Greek word meaning "easy death." Euthanasia is the direct killing of a person who is disabled, sick, or dying. It also goes by the name "mercy killing." Pope John Paul II defines euthanasia as any "action or omission which of itself and by intention causes death, with the purpose of eliminating all suffering" (*The Gospel of Life,* 65). Direct euthanasia is murder. It gravely violates the dignity of a human person and does not respect God, the Author of Life.

People who are disabled or very sick and who are suffering deserve our care and respect. We are to support them medically, psychologically, and spiritually to help them lead as normal a life as possible. We must always use the "ordinary" medical means available to care for our own lives and the lives of others.

We are, however, not required to use "extraordinary means" to care for ourselves or others. Such extraordinary means would include dangerous and burdensome medical procedures or expenses.

Listening to the Word of God

Read and reflect on the Scripture verses listed in the right column. Match the descriptions in the left column with the teaching of the verses.

____ 1. God will demand an accounting of anyone who sheds the blood of another.

____ 2. Never kill an innocent person.

____ 3. Do not be angry with anyone.

____ 4. God has always known us, even before we were born.

____ 5. Those who lead others to sin deserve a terrible fate.

____ 6. God will bless those who are dedicated to peace.

A. Exodus 23:7

B. Jeremiah 1:5

C. Matthew 5:9

D. Genesis 9:5–6

E. Matthew 5:21–26

F. Matthew 18:6

It is morally permissible for us to use painkillers to reduce suffering, even if such medical treatment might shorten a person's natural life. We may use such medication only for the lessening of pain and not with the intention of directly causing death.

Suicide

Freely created by God, we must honor and respect the gift of our life. We are stewards, not owners, of our lives. God alone is the sovereign of human life. To kill oneself, suicide, is a serious lack of love toward oneself, one's family, and the human community. It is a serious lack of love and trust in God the Father, Son, and Holy Spirit, who is always present with us in all our joys and sufferings.

Suicide, the taking of one's own life, is seriously contrary to the virtues of justice, hope, and charity. It is a grave violation of the fifth commandment. To support or cooperate in another person's decision to commit suicide or to assist another person in committing suicide—assisted suicide—is gravely wrong. It is also a serious violation against God's command not to kill.

Factors like grave psychological problems, extreme fear in anticipating suffering, or torture can reduce one's blameworthiness for the sin of suicide. We should pray for persons who see life as so bleak that they decide to end it.

Respect for the Dignity of Persons

Respect is defined as "esteem, honor, or showing appreciation." We **respect** God's gift of life by honoring others and ourselves by respecting the lives of each and every person without exception. These are some specific moral teachings that flow from this moral principle, which lies at the foundation of the fifth commandment.

Spiritual Life of Others

Scandal leads another to do evil. It works at destroying the spiritual life of others. Scandal is especially wrong if teachers, elected officials, coaches, and others whom we respect—because they are entrusted with our well-being— lead us into sin. Lawmakers can be guilty of scandal by promoting or allowing social conditions that lead to a decline in morals. Business fraud and media promotions of immorality are a growing source of scandal in our society. Whatever our role in society, we need to be aware of the power of good example, the true antidote to scandal.

Healthy Lifestyle

We respect God's gift of life to us through a healthy lifestyle. We have the responsibility to choose foods and activities that contribute to our physical and emotional health.

Society has a responsibility to help us meet this responsibility. Its laws should guarantee the basic rights to food, shelter, clothing, health care, education, employment, and social security.

We respect our life when we avoid the misuse of food, alcohol, and tobacco. The worship of physical beauty and bodily perfection or the "building of bodies" to achieve success in sports at all costs is not a sign of respect or honor for oneself. Pursuing such a "cult of the body" leads to prejudice against the weak or physically challenged and results in perverted human relationships.

We also live responsibly when we do not abuse prescription and over-the-counter drugs and when we do not use or sell illegal drugs. We also respect life when we avoid harmful driving practices that endanger human lives.

Medical and Scientific Research

Medical and scientific research, which is continuously unlocking the secrets of nature, has the special mission to heal and advance public health. When we use procedures discovered through medical and scientific research, we must always respect the dignity of the human person. Medical experimentation and organ transplants must respect human dignity, promote the common good, and only be used with the informed consent of donors and patients. Organ transplants are morally acceptable if the risks to the donor are proportionate to the good gained by the recipient of a transplanted organ.

Integrity of the Human Body

The New Testament teaches that we are Temples of the Holy Spirit. We respect the bodies of both the living and the dead. Certain acts seriously violate the integrity of the human body. Kidnapping, terrorism, hostage taking, and physical and psychological torture show grave disregard for and victimize people. While some groups and even nations justify these loathsome acts as necessary to defend themselves or to maintain an orderly society, they assault human dignity and are always contrary to the fifth commandment.

Such practices arise out of hate and revenge and are seriously contrary to the virtues of charity and justice. In addition, they cost societies inordinate amounts of money for self-protection—sums that could go to the care of the poor.

We are also to work for the abolition of amputation, mutilation, and steriliza-tion performed on innocent people. Such procedures are against the moral law unless they are performed for legit-imate therapeutic medical reasons to save the lives of patients. They gravely offend God's Law when used for any other reason.

Caring for the Dying and the Dead

In the Apostles' Creed, we profess our faith in "the resurrection of the body, and the life everlasting." This truth is a fundamental belief of Christian faith.

We live out this truth of our faith when we respect life and honor people who are dying by helping them face death with dignity and peace. We also honor those who have died when we lovingly care for and bury their bodies. Cremating the body of someone who has died is morally acceptable if it is not done to deny the truth of the resurrection of the body.

(CCC, 2302–2317)

Working for Peace

Jesus calls us to peace. People living in peace and justice are signs of the kingdom of God announced and proclaimed by Jesus.

Anger and Hatred

In the Sermon on the Mount, Jesus teaches, "Blessed are the peacemakers, / for they will be called children of God" (Matthew 5:9). At the bare minimum, living as a peacemaker requires each of us to root hatred and the desire for revenge from our hearts. These can easily lead to the harming, even the killing, of our "neighbor," whom Jesus commands us to love as we love ourselves. Deliberate hatred is opposed to Christian love. It is also contrary to the peace and reconcilia-tion preached and lived by Jesus, who taught, "But I say to you, whoever is angry with his brother will be liable to judgment" (Matthew 5:22).

Respect Life

The fifth commandment calls us to appreciate, respect, and cherish the precious gift of life that God gave to each of us. One important way we do this is by trying our best to live a healthy life—physically, psychologically, and spiritually. Examine how well you are doing by evaluating yourself in each of the following areas. Use this scale:

> A = I'm doing an excellent job
> B = very good
> C = average
> D = poor
> F = flunking (I need a lot of work on this area)

Physical health

_____ 1. I eat healthful foods, including fruits and vegetables, on a daily basis.

_____ 2. I get plenty of sleep each night.

_____ 3. I avoid the use of recreational drugs, including the drinking of alcohol.

_____ 4. I exercise on a regular basis.

Psychological health

_____ 5. I spend time cultivating friendships.

_____ 6. I have a variety of hobbies or interests.

_____ 7. I am affectionate with my loved ones and allow them to show affection to me.

_____ 8. I have someone to confide in when I am troubled.

Spiritual health

_____ 9. I confess my sins when I need God's forgiveness.

_____ 10. I pray regularly.

_____ 11. I take part in Sunday liturgy and receive Holy Communion regularly.

_____ 12. I read the Bible regularly.

_____ **How would you grade your overall effort in caring for the gift of life that God gave to you?**

List two other "healthy" practices that you engage in to cultivate the beautiful gift of life that God gave to you. Share your responses with your group.

Journal Writing: Identify one area of your life that needs the most work *right now*. Write what concrete action you can do during the next two weeks to work on that area. How will you check back at the end of the two weeks to evaluate your effort?

War

Jesus has reconciled us with God. He is our model of reconciling with others. The Church, the Body of Christ, is both a sign and an instrument of the reconciliation. True peace results when individuals and nations work toward the peaceful and nonviolent reconciliation of their disagreements. True peace is the fruit of free communication among people and respecting the dignity of others and their goods.

War is the violent settling of differences. Some Christians are against war on principle. The Church praises peacemakers who renounce violence and witness to love, as long as they do so without harming the rights of others.

The Church also recognizes the right of governments to defend their citizens against unjust aggression by engaging in a "just war" after all peace efforts have failed. Because of the evils and injustices that all war brings upon people, we must do everything that is reasonably possible to avoid war.

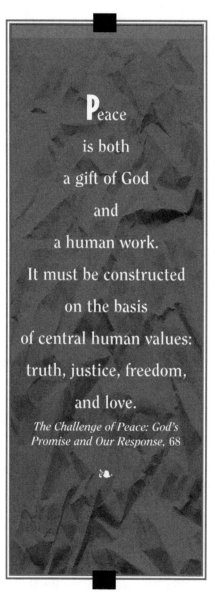

Peace

is both

a gift of God

and

a human work.

It must be constructed

on the basis

of central human values:

truth, justice, freedom,

and love.

The Challenge of Peace: God's Promise and Our Response, 68

When a nation participates in a "just war," the moral law demanding respect for the dignity of people remains in effect.

❑ The military must humanely treat and respect wounded soldiers, prisoners, and noncombatants.

❑ Belligerents must honor the laws of nations and universal principles of humanity. Therefore, war participants must never blindly obey any efforts to wipe out a people, nation, or ethnic minority. Genocide is a crime against humanity that we must always resist.

❑ The indiscriminate destruction of entire cities or inhabited regions is a crime against God and humanity.

❑ Modern biological, chemical, and atomic weapons cannot discriminate between combatants and innocent citizens. It is very difficult to ever justify their use.

Authorities, however, should provide alternative forms of service for persons who object to bearing arms. The Catholic Church acknowledges conscientious objection to war. Those who refuse to bear arms must still serve the community in another way.

The Arms Race

Military strategists believe that it is necessary to stockpile weapons in order to deter other nations from attacking. The Church, however, seriously questions the arms race and describes it as "one of the greatest curses on the human race and the harm it inflicts on the poor is more than can be endured" (*Pastoral Constitution on the Church in the Modern World*, 81).

The theory of deterrence neither ensures peace nor eliminates the causes of war. In addition, the production and sale of arms negatively affect the common good of nations and the international community. Money spent on arms gravely violates our responsibility for meeting the basic human needs of people living in poverty and hinders the development of peoples. The profit motive cannot outweigh the violence and conflict that arms-dealing fosters.

We fight the evil of war best and most effectively by working for justice. We do so by rooting out excessive economic and social inequalities and by fighting envy, greed, pride, and distrust among peoples. Jesus has shown us the way to be a peacemaker: We are to serve others. Imitating Jesus is the great antidote to the hate and anger that engender war.

Can Christians fight in a war?

Because nations have the right to self-defense, they and their Christian citizens may engage in a "just war." A nation's legitimate authorities must very seriously weigh the following factors. *All* must be present simultaneously for a war to be just:

- The damage inflicted by the aggressor on the nation or community of nations must be lasting, grave, and certain;

- all other means of putting an end to their disputes must have been shown to be impractical or ineffective;

- there must be serious prospects of success;

- the use of arms must not produce evils and disorders graver than the evil to be eliminated. The power of modern means of destruction weighs very heavily in evaluating this condition. (See CCC, 2309.)

Discuss:
Can there be a just nuclear war?

Peace Prayer of Saint Francis of Assisi

Lord, make me an instrument
  of your peace:
where there is hatred,
  let me sow love;
where there is injury, pardon;
where there is doubt, faith;
where there is despair, hope;
where there is darkness, light;
where there is sadness, joy.

O divine Master,
  grant that I may not so much
    seek
to be consoled as to console,
to be understood
  as to understand,
to be loved as to love.
For it is in giving that we
  receive,
it is in pardoning that we are
  pardoned,
it is in dying that we are
  born to eternal life.

Amen.

REVIEW

IMPORTANT TERMS TO KNOW

abortion—the direct, deliberate, intentional killing of an embryo or nonviable fetus using medical or surgical procedures. Because it kills innocent human life, direct abortion is a grave violation of the fifth commandment.

arms race—the stockpiling of weapons as a way of deterring aggression against a country

euthanasia—any "action or omission which of itself and by intention causes death, with the purpose of eliminating all suffering" (*Gospel of Life*, 65)

murder—the killing of an innocent person

scandal—an "attitude or behavior which leads another to do evil" (CCC, 2284)

suicide—the taking of one's own life

CHAPTER SUMMARY

Every human's life, from the moment of conception until death, is sacred. God is the Author of Life and has created us in his image and likeness. In this chapter we learned:

1. The fifth commandment teaches that we must respect and honor all human life. The murder of a human being is gravely contrary to the dignity of the person and the holiness of the Creator.

2. Legitimate self-defense is both a right and a grave duty for whoever is responsible for the lives of others or the common good.

3. Societies may engage in just wars and inflict the death penalty on capital criminals as a last resort. Kidnapping, terrorism, hostage taking, torture, and amputations (except to save someone's life) are serious attacks on the sacredness of human life.

4. Direct abortion is gravely contrary to the moral law. The Church imposes the canonical penalty of excommunication for this crime against human life.

5. Euthanasia is murder. Sick and suffering people deserve respect, compassion, prayer, and ordinary care to sustain their lives.

6. Suicide is the taking of one's own life. It is the equivalent of murder. We can never justify it.

7. Scandal is seriously sinful if it leads someone to commit serious sin.

8. We must do everything reasonably possible to avoid war. Under very strict conditions, as a last resort, a nation has the right to engage in a just war of self-defense.

9. ". . . the arms race is one of the greatest curses on the human race . . ." (*Pastoral Constitution on the Church in the Modern World*, 81).

10. We should help dying people do so in dignity and peace. We should honor corpses and bury the dead with respect, thus showing our belief in the resurrection of the body.

EXPLORING OUR CATHOLIC FAITH

1. Listening to God's Word

Read and reflect on Matthew 5:21–22. In what way does this teaching of Jesus help you understand the meaning of the fifth commandment?

2. Understanding the Teachings of the Catholic Church

The bishops at the Second Vatican Council taught, "It is our clear duty to spare no effort in order to work for the moment when all war will be completely outlawed by international agreement" (*Pastoral Constitution on the Church in the Modern World,* 82). Why do you think the Church has set this goal?

3. Reflecting on Our Catholic Faith

G. K. Chesterton in *Orthodoxy* wrote, "Not only is suicide a sin, it is the sin. It is the ultimate and absolute evil, the refusal to take the oath of loyalty to life." Reflect on your dignity and the sacredness of life. Write your thoughts in your journal.

4. Living Our Catholic Faith

Someone wrote, "The drunkard commits suicide and murder on the installment plan." Teenagers around the United States are rallying against drunken driving. Name ways you can participate in this effort, or in any other effort that works to respect and protect human life.

CHAPTER 8

The Sixth and Ninth Commandments: Respect Sexuality

Do you not know that your body is a temple of the holy Spirit within you, whom you have from God, and that you are not your own? For you have been purchased at a price. Therefore glorify God in your body.

1 CORINTHIANS 6: 19–20

Reflect on this teaching of the Church:

> Every baptized person is called to live a chaste life, according to one's particular state of life.

What does this teaching mean to you? Write your ideas in this space.

One of O. Henry's most popular short stories is *The Gift of the Magi.* A young married couple who are deeply in love are living in New York City at the turn of the century. It is Christmas time and each one wants to find that special gift for the other. But they do not have much extra spending money; in fact they are poor. So she sells her long beautiful hair to buy a watch chain for his most prized possession, his pocket watch. He sells his gold pocket watch to buy combs for her most prized possession, her hair. She is so excited about her gift that she does not wait until Christmas to give it to him. Then they both realize what each one did. The combs and the watch chain are gently placed into a drawer as silent, but very tangible reminders of the love that flowed from their deep respect for each other.

Respect is fundamental to every human relationship.

KEY TERMS
adultery

chastity

concupiscence

contraception

divorce

fornication

free union

lust

modesty

pornography

Our sexual drive is the powerful urge that God implanted in us to fulfill our responsibility to "[b]e fertile and multiply" (Genesis 1:28). But, like so many powers, we can use this power to hurt ourselves and other people. In this chapter we will look at how the sixth commandment and the ninth commandment encompass all areas of human sexuality. They teach us how to relate sexually to others in a responsible, moral, godly, and life-giving way. These commandments promote three virtues—chastity, purity, and modesty—that help us live according to God's plan.

(*Catechism of the Catholic Church*, 2331–2350, 2514–2527)

The Mystery of Human Love and Communion

God created human beings in his image. "God is love and in himself he lives a mystery of personal loving communion. Creating the human race in his own image . . . God inscribed in the humanity of man and woman the vocation, and thus the capacity and responsibility, of love and communion" (*On the Family*, 11).

Human Sexuality

God created humans, male and female, out of love and for love. "Each of the two sexes is an image of the power and tenderness of God, with equal dignity though in a different way" (CCC, 2335).

Each of us is called to acknowledge and respect our sexuality because it affects all aspects of who we are. Our sexuality especially concerns our capacity to love and procreate, and to form relationships with others. Marriage and family life, which is the basis for a harmonious society, is built on our complementary nature as female and male. The union of woman and man in marriage imitates the personal loving communion that unites God—Father, Son, and Holy Spirit.

The Virtue of Chastity

We have the responsibility to acknowledge and accept our sexual identity in a chaste way. With personal effort and the help of the Holy Spirit, we can learn how to be chaste. We can learn to use the beautiful powers of life and love given to us by God in a truly human way.

Chastity is a moral virtue and a grace. It helps us lead a life that is a sign of God's fidelity and loving kindness. The chaste person uses the powers of life and love both to maintain his or her own integrity as a person and to appropriately offer himself or herself as a gift to another person.

Chastity involves our integrity as a person. It teaches us and empowers us to use our freedom to master our sexual powers so that we are not dominated and enslaved by them. Mastering our sexual drives is a difficult and lifelong task, from adolescence through old age. It is also a task that requires the support of a society that respects human dignity, cherishes wholesome sex education, and supports family life.

Striving for Chastity

A Reflection

As we grow to maturity, we often feel that our vocation to live sexually upright lives is impossible. Sometimes we fall short of his call and feel depressed about our weakness. However, we must always remember that Jesus was human. He knows what it means for us to struggle to live a chaste, Christian life.

The Lord's grace is always available to help us. For example, he will strengthen us in prayer. He graces us with the sacraments, forgiving our failures in the sacrament of Confession and giving us himself for strength in the Eucharist. He reaches out to us through the Christian community, especially older and wiser Christian friends and relatives who have been striving to be chaste for years. We should never fear to approach a trusted adult (parent, priest, teacher) and ask for their advice and support.

True, Christ Jesus calls us to high standards. But he gives us help to reach them. If we fall short, we should never hate ourselves. Rather, we should look at these setbacks as opportunities to grow, to learn, and to experience the forgiveness and love of the Lord. He will always be with us on our journey.

In baptism, we have put on Christ, the model of chastity, and have been called to live a life of chastity. We do this in keeping with our state in life. Members of religious communities live chaste lives when they abstain from sexual activity. Married men and women live chaste lives when they are faithful to each other and use their sexual powers to show love and share life. Similarly, single people and engaged couples live chaste lives when they exercise self-control and wait until they are married to engage in intimate sexual relations.

Living a chaste life is not something we can achieve totally by willpower. It is also a grace, a gift of the Holy Spirit. The Spirit strengthens us to master ourselves and give witness to God's love and fidelity. He helps us form true friendships that teach us the meaning of spiritual communion. Through the Church, the Spirit teaches us some excellent ways to gain sexual self-control. These include:

❏ resisting temptations by avoiding those situations that might lead us to sin, for example, looking at pornographic materials;

❏ growing in honest self-knowledge;

❏ engaging in works of self-discipline to build up our character;

❏ obeying God's commandments;

❏ practicing the moral virtues;

❏ praying for help to gain self-mastery;

❏ frequently receiving the sacraments of Penance and the Eucharist.

The Pure of Heart

Jesus taught, "Blessed are the clean of heart,/for they will see God" (Matthew 5:8). We are "pure of heart" if we place God first in our lives and attune our "intellects and wills to the demands of God's holiness" (CCC, 2518).

When we do, we begin to see "as God sees." We see ourselves and others as images of God and temples of the Holy Spirit. The pure of heart strive to live according to the demands of God's holiness. Purity of heart includes three things: charity, chastity, and love of the truth and orthodoxy of faith.

The Virtues of Modesty and Purity

The ninth commandment promotes the virtues of purity and **modesty.** The virtue of purity helps us seek to find and fulfill God's will above all else. The virtue of modesty "encourages patience and moderation in loving relationships; it requires that the conditions for the definitive giving and commitment of man and woman to one another be fulfilled." It requires discretion and "inspires one's choice of clothing" (CCC, 2522). Modesty protects the intimate center of the person. It guides us in how we look at and behave toward others.

The virtues of modesty and purity help us live chaste lives and combat covetousness or **concupiscence**. Catholic theology defines concupiscence as "an inordinate desire of our sense appetites contrary to human reason. It results from original sin and inclines us to commit sin." Saint Paul referred to it as the "Spirit" warring against the "flesh."

> I say, then: live by the Spirit and you will certainly not gratify the desire of the flesh. For the flesh has desires against the Spirit, and the Spirit against the flesh; these are opposed to each other, so that you may not do what you want.
>
> **Galatians 5:16–17**

Concupiscence leads to the vice of **lust,** which works against our living chaste lives. Lust is the disordered craving for sexual pleasure for its own sake—isolated from its unitive (love) and procreative functions intended by God only for husband and wife. What lust does is turn people into objects of pleasure.

We distinguish between lust and sexual thoughts and desires that are normal and wholesome. Sexual thoughts become lustful when we become obsessed with them, allowing them to control us. They are lustful when we look on others as mere objects of self-pleasure and not as persons to be loved.

Our struggle against lust, or carnal concupiscence, as well as purifying our heart and practicing temperance take constant effort and cooperation with God's grace on our part. We receive a pure heart at baptism. We are reborn of water and the Spirit as adopted sons and daughters of God. Purity of heart attunes our hearts and minds to God's holiness.

However, living as a person with a "pure heart" requires God's grace and constant effort on our part. We grow as a person with a pure heart by practicing chastity and by seeking to do God's will through self-discipline and prayer.

(CCC, 2351–2359)

Actions Contrary to the Virtue of Chastity

Sins that are gravely contrary to chastity are masturbation, fornication, pornography, prostitution, rape, and homosexuality.

Masturbation is the deliberate stimulation of the genital organs to seek sexual pleasure. Masturbation is contrary to our living a chaste life because sexual pleasure is sought outside the sexual union of marriage. To judge whether a person is guilty of grave sin, however, requires caution and wisdom. The *Catechism of the Catholic Church* teaches:

> To form an equitable judgment about the subjects' moral responsibility and to guide pastoral action, one must take into account the affective immaturity, force of acquired habit, conditions of anxiety, or other psychological or social factors that lessen or even extenuate moral culpability (2352).

Fornication is sexual union between an unmarried man and an unmarried woman. **Fornication** is gravely wrong because it violates God's intention for sexual intercourse to express the total love and openness to life that we find in marriage alone. Premarital sexual intercourse, including sexual intercourse between engaged couples, seeks pleasure without this responsibility; it is an expression of a serious failure to "love." The gravity of fornication is increased when it gives scandal to the young.

Pornography debases the holiness of sexual relations and degrades people by turning them into objects of the debased sexual pleasure of others. **Pornography** assaults the dignity of those who create it, sell it, or use it to inflame their sexual passions. Society should outlaw the making and selling of pornography in any form: pictures, magazines, books, videos, and so forth.

Prostitution is the selling of a person's body for the sexual pleasure of another. It gravely violates human dignity, making the prostitute a mere object, and cheapens God's gift of sexual intercourse given for the expression of intimate love between husband and wife and the procreation of children. The person who pays for prostitution is involved in a serious sin against chastity, defiling his own body, a temple of the Holy Spirit. Women are usually thought of as prostitutes, but men, children, and adolescents also "prostitute" themselves. Although prostitution is gravely wrong, a person's blameworthiness can be lessened because of poverty, blackmail, or social pressure. Society should recognize the scourge that prostitution really is by outlawing it.

Rape is an act of violence and injustice. It is the "forcible violation of the sexual intimacy of another person" (CCC, 2356). Rape is an intrinsically and gravely evil act. It violates a person's sexuality and integrity and offends the virtues of justice and love. Graver still is the sexual assault of children by parents (incest) or by trusted adults because of the added violation of the trust that unites children and parents and children and teachers. All rape is gravely wrong and psychologically maims the victims for life, affecting the self-respect, freedom, and physical and moral wholeness to which everyone has a right.

Homosexuality. The Church distinguishes between a *homosexual orientation* and *homosexual acts*. A homosexual orientation is the exclusive or predominant sexual attraction to a member of the same sex. Christ calls homosexual persons to be chaste, just as he calls all people to be chaste. Homosexual acts are gravely wrong. They frustrate God's purpose for human sexual sharing: the unity of a husband and wife and the openness to the procreation of human life.

Marriage

According to God's plan, the marriage covenant is an intimate communion of life and love between a man and a woman. It has been endowed with its own special laws by the Creator. By its very nature it is ordered to the good of the couple, as well as the generation and education of children.

Sexual intercourse between a woman and man who are married is a sign of total giving, a pledge of unconditional love. The gift of sexual sharing brings both joy and pleasure to the couple; the two are united as one in love. Their union results in two outcomes: the mutual good between them and the transmission of human life.

The Marriage Covenant

The marriage between a baptized man and woman is a sacrament. It signifies the union of Christ and the Church.

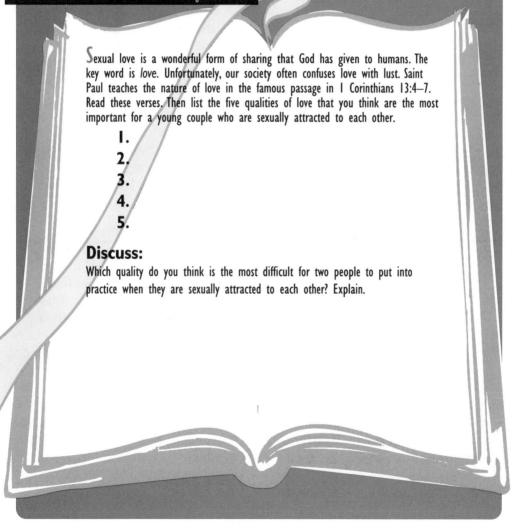

The Word of God in My Life

Sexual love is a wonderful form of sharing that God has given to humans. The key word is *love*. Unfortunately, our society often confuses love with lust. Saint Paul teaches the nature of love in the famous passage in 1 Corinthians 13:4–7. Read these verses. Then list the five qualities of love that you think are the most important for a young couple who are sexually attracted to each other.

1.
2.
3.
4.
5.

Discuss:
Which quality do you think is the most difficult for two people to put into practice when they are sexually attracted to each other? Explain.

It is a sign of Christ's unconditional love for his Body, the Church. The spouses receive the grace to live their marriage covenant.

The marriage of a husband and wife is a covenant that reflects Christ's total, permanent, unconditional, selfless love for us. It requires both fidelity and fecundity.

Fidelity. Married couples build their marriage upon faithful love. The couple promise to be faithful and loyal to each other until death. Just as God is unconditionally faithful to us and Christ is unconditionally faithful to the Church, a married couple must live a life of fidelity, or faithfulness to each other. For this reason a true marriage is indissoluble. By keeping their word, a baptized married couple image God's faithful love to people and Christ's faithful love for the Church.

Fecundity. The sharing of love and the transmission of life are the two purposes of marriage. A married couple share in God's creative power. They have the privilege and responsibility to procreate, to cooperate with God in the giving of new life. Because this is so, the Church teaches that "each and every marriage act must remain open to the transmission of life" (*Of Human Life*, 11).

Responsible cooperation with God's plan requires careful thought in family planning. For just and unselfish reasons, a couple may limit the number and spacing of their children. Just and unselfish reasons include the physical and psychological health of a spouse, family finances, and the good of the family. Morally acceptable birth regulation safeguards both the unitive (love-sharing) and procreative (life-sharing) aspects of sexual intercourse.

The Church teaches and recognizes that regulation of births is an important responsibility of married life. Sexual intercourse must be open to the sharing of love and the transmission of life. **Contraception** uses morally unacceptable methods of birth control, such as the medical procedures of tube tying and vasectomy and the use of pills and condoms, to directly prevent the transmission of life. Because such contraceptive means directly aim to frustrate this essential purpose of sexual intercourse, they are contrary to God's will.

Periodically abstaining from sexual intercourse and natural family planning (NFP) are means that respect and protect both aspects of sexual intercourse. These methods help promote true human freedom and encourage tenderness, sensitivity, and good communication between spouses. All these are key ingredients to nurturing faithful love between spouses.

Some couples are sterile, that is, unable to have children. There are morally acceptable medical means available to reduce their sterility. Couples may use such means; however, techniques such as the donation of sperm or an egg, or the use of a surrogate uterus, are seriously wrong and may not be used. These violate the exclusive union of the married couple. Other techniques, such as artificial insemination, involve only the married couple. Catholic morality forbids such techniques because they separate the act of intercourse from the act of procreation.

We can only fully understand the meaning of human life and its transmission from the point of view of who we are and of our eternal destiny. As persons of faith, we know life is God's gift. We are created in the image and likeness of God. We are called into friendship with him forever. A child—indeed, every human life—is a gift. Married couples have the privilege and responsibility from God to take part in the procreation of new life through the sharing of their life and love with each other.

One of the few places in the Gospels where Jesus addresses an issue of sexual morality involves a woman caught in adultery. The way he dealt with it was to clearly name the sin, call the woman to repentance, and forgive her sin.

Read John 8:1–11 and answer the questions below.

1. Who accused the woman of adultery?

2. What did the Mosaic Law command about such a sin?

3. What did Jesus say to her accusers?

4. What did Jesus say to the woman?

Discuss: Why do you think movies, television sitcoms, and talk shows do not portray adultery as "morally wrong" or simply portray it as morally acceptable?

Offenses against the Marriage Covenant

Adultery, divorce, polygamy, incest, and free union are grave offenses against the dignity of marriage. Each undermines and destroys the lifelong and exclusive faithful love that is at the heart of the marriage covenant.

Adultery is sexual relations between married persons and someone other than their spouse. **Adultery** is a grave injustice to the marriage covenant in which the partners promised lifelong fidelity. It disrupts family life, causes harm to the innocent spouse and the children, and leads to disharmony in society. So serious an offense is adultery that Jesus even forbade lust, adultery of the heart.

Divorce is the legal dissolution of a ratified and consummated marriage. **Divorce** seeks to break the covenant of lifelong fidelity and commitment that is freely and knowingly entered into by spouses.

In some difficult cases, such as those involving the safety and health of the children and spouse, the Church will permit a civil divorce. The marriage, however, still exists, and the couple are still sacramentally married. The separated spouses must not engage in sexual relations with others or enter into another marriage.

Though we recognize divorce as a sign of a serious failure to love, we should refrain from judging divorced couples. Life is complex and difficult. God is a forgiving God. We need to support and love those who are suffering.

The Church calls on all married people to work out their problems through communication, prayers, closeness to Jesus in the sacraments, and counseling. Likewise, the Church community supports the victims of divorce as they try to heal their wounds of self-hatred, doubt, anger, and confusion.

Polygamy is having more than one marriage partner. It contradicts God's law that a marriage is a unique and exclusive love union between one man and one woman.

Incest is engaging in sexual relations with close relatives or in-laws. Related to incest is any kind of sexual abuse of children or adolescents in the care of adults.

Free union is living together without committing to marriage vows. Similar to so-called "trial marriages," in which couples claim they will marry later, these "unions" lack the total and exclusive commitment of love proclaimed by a public marriage.

To engage in sex outside marriage is to misuse seriously the language of love that speaks of exclusive and unconditional union. It is mortally sinful "and excludes one from sacramental communion" with the Body of Christ, the Church (CCC, 2390).

> Do not conform yourself
> to this age
> but be transformed
> by the renewal of your mind,
> that you may discern
> what is the will of God,
> what is good and
> pleasing and perfect.
> **Romans 12:2**

Marriage Blessing

Priest: May almighty God, with his Word of blessing, unite your hearts in the never-ending bond of pure love.

All: Amen.

Priest: May your children bring you happiness, and may your generous love for them be returned to you, many times over.

All: Amen.

Priest: May the peace of Christ live always in your hearts and in your home.

May you have true friends to stand by you, both in joy and in sorrow.

May you be ready and willing to help and comfort all who come to you in need.

And may the blessings promised to the compassionate be yours in abundance.

All: Amen.

Rite of Marriage

IMPORTANT TERMS TO KNOW

adultery—sexual intercourse between a married person and someone who is not the person's spouse

chastity—the virtue that enables us to act morally in sexual matters according to our station in life

concupiscence—an inordinate desire or covetousness, especially for sexual pleasures or another's material goods

contraception—a free act involving some artificial means, such as the use of birth control pills, that interferes with sexual intercourse in order to prevent conception

divorce—the legal dissolving of a marriage

fornication—sexual intercourse between a man and a woman who are not married

free union—living together without committing to marriage vows

lust—the disordered desire for or inordinate enjoyment of sexual pleasure

modesty—the virtue of temperance as it applies to one's speech, dress, personal life, and the like. Flowing from purity, it protects one's most intimate self, refusing to unveil what should remain covered.

pornography—the description of sexual acts with the purpose of arousing immoral sexual feelings

CHAPTER SUMMARY

1. God created us male and female—sexual beings—out of love and for love. Our sexual nature orders our capacity to love and procreate.

2. The virtue of chastity integrates our sexuality with our person and uses it morally according to our situation in life. Serious offenses against chastity include masturbation, fornication, pornography, rape, homosexuality, and prostitution.

3. Rape is an intrinsically evil act that seriously violates a person's sexuality and integrity. It is never morally justifiable.

4. Sexual concupiscence leads to lust, the disordered craving for sexual pleasure. The struggle against carnal lust involves purifying the heart and practicing temperance.

5. Purity of heart requires us to focus our hearts and minds on God's holiness. It calls us to practice decency, discretion, and modesty, which protects the intimate center of the person.

6. Church teaching distinguishes between homosexual orientation and homosexual acts. Homosexual orientation is not sinful. Christ calls homosexual persons to be chaste, just as he calls all people to be chaste. Because homosexual acts frustrate the aims of marriage, they are seriously wrong.

7. Sexual intercourse is ordered to the total giving in love of married partners and to the transmission of new life. Marriage is a lifelong covenant that mirrors Christ's unconditional love for his Church. It requires both fidelity and fecundity.

8. Contraception is a serious offense against God's plan for sexual sharing and the transmission of life. Adultery, divorce, polygamy, incest, and free union (trial marriages) all seriously offend against the dignity of marriage. Medicine may provide moral means to help sterile couples. However, techniques such as using a surrogate uterus or donated sperm or ova, or any method of artificial insemination, are immoral.

EXPLORING OUR CATHOLIC FAITH

1. Listening to God's Word

Read 1 Corinthians 6:19–20. How do these words of Scripture help guide us in living our relationships with each other?

2. Understanding the Teachings of the Catholic Church

The *Catechism of the Catholic Church* teaches, "Each of the two sexes is an image of the power and tenderness of God, with equal dignity though in a different way" (2335). What does this teaching mean? How does it guide you?

3. Reflecting on Our Catholic Faith

Saint Bernard of Clairvaux, a doctor of the Church who lived from 1091 to 1153, wrote, "Inordinate love of the flesh is cruelty, because under the appearance of pleasing the body we kill the soul." Explain why you agree or disagree with this insight.

4. Living Our Catholic Faith

The Catholic Church teaches that all rape is a violent act of injustice and is always gravely wrong. Yet, of seventeen hundred students interviewed, a majority stated that it is all right for a man to force a woman to have sexual relations if the couple have been dating for six months or more. How would you respond to these youths?

CHAPTER 9

The Seventh and Tenth Commandments: Live Justly

Defend the lowly and fatherless;
render justice to the afflicted and needy.
PSALM 82:3

What does it mean to act justly?

KEY TERMS

almsgiving

avarice

covetousness

envy

greed

justice

social justice teaching

stewardship

Works of Mercy

Not too long ago, a teenager was sitting on a crowded bus, studying for a major history exam. Noticing an elderly lady standing near him, he stood up and politely offered his seat to her. The elderly lady's eyes widened in amazement. She dropped her packages and suddenly slumped, fainting on the spot.

When she revived seconds later, she looked kindly into the face of the thoughtful teen who had surrendered his seat. "Thank you," she said.

At this unexpected expression of gratitude, the teen fainted.

Common courtesy and the expression of gratitude sometimes bring surprise and shock. Why is that?

The Gospel calls us to treat others with respect, justice, and love. We should always show a ready willingness to share with others, to give them their just due, to respond to their needs. In this chapter we will be studying the seventh and tenth commandments. We will discuss our responsibility to treat others fairly and how to respect all the gifts God has bestowed on us.

(*Catechism of the Catholic Church,* 2401–2407, 2534–2550)

Justice and Charity

Justice and charity are at the heart of our stewardship of, or responsibility to care for, creation and material goods. The seventh commandment reminds us that God created earthly goods for the benefit of all people. It instructs us to be just persons who respect the rights of others by "rendering them their due." It forbids theft, the taking or keeping of another's goods, and defrauding our neighbor in any way concerning his or her possessions.

This command not only teaches us that people have the right to own private property and to enjoy the rewards of their work, but it also names our responsibilities toward those goods. Ownership of goods is meant for the common good of all and not merely for our own personal benefit. Furthermore, this command of the Decalogue requires the virtue of solidarity, which calls us to share our wealth and goods with others, especially with people who are poor and needy.

The Virtue of Temperance

Our desire to own possessions that give us pleasure is natural and good—but we must seek and use those possessions justly. The virtue of temperance guides us in using and seeking created and material goods. We practice temperance so that we become the master of our possessions and they do not enslave us. The tenth commandment warns us to keep the desire for possessions within the bonds of reason and to avoid "coveting" unjustly what belongs to another.

Covetousness

We must always seek and obtain our possessions in a just and fair way. The tenth commandment forbids **covetousness,** which the Catholic tradition has also called "lust of the eyes." Simply desiring to have what another person might own does not violate the tenth commandment; but desiring, or coveting, another person's possession out of **greed, avarice,** and **envy** does. The sins of greed, avarice, and envy—sins of the heart—lead to the external sins that the seventh commandment forbids.

Greed and avarice. Greed drives us to amass more and more wealth regardless of the needs of others. An avaricious person passionately tries to get riches and the power that comes with them. Avarice makes a god out of possessions. It is the root of fraud, theft, and robbery—all of which the seventh commandment outlaws.

Envy. Envy is the inordinate desire for another's goods, even leading to unjust means to acquire them. People motivated by envy are sad that others have something they do not own. The evil of envy is increased—and can be mortally sinful—if we hope for serious harm to come to the person whose goods we covet. The evil of envy is further magnified when the excessive love and pursuit of wealth and possessions leads to idolatry—we end up worshiping created goods rather than their Creator.

Jesus knew the human heart very well. He taught us that detachment from riches is necessary for entering the kingdom of heaven. He taught:

> "Do not store up for yourselves treasures on earth, where moth and decay destroys, and thieves break in and steal. But store up treasures in heaven, where neither moth nor decay destroy, nor thieves break in and steal. For where your treasure is, there also will your heart be."
> **Matthew 6:19–21**

The Spirit, the giver of life, guides and strengthens us to trust in the providence of God. Through humility and goodwill we can keep what is really important before our eyes—our union with God—and keep our pursuit and use of material goods in perspective.

Christians don't own their wealth—they owe it.

Jesus often addressed our pursuit and use of material possessions. Read Matthew 19:16–30.

What is God saying to you?

What difference might these words have in the decisions you make, both now and in the future?

Respect for Another's Property

When we respect another person's property, we are actually showing respect for that person—not just his or her goods. The seventh commandment teaches this type of respect of others by forbidding theft, slavery, and immoral gambling.

- ❏ business fraud
- ❏ paying unjust wages
- ❏ price fixing
- ❏ corruption that illegally or immorally influences lawmakers
- ❏ theft of the common goods of an enterprise
- ❏ inferior work
- ❏ tax evasion
- ❏ expense account padding
- ❏ wasteful practices
- ❏ forgery of checks and invoices
- ❏ damaging private or public property

Theft

Theft is the taking of the property of another person against the reasonable will of that person. When we steal another person's property, we are, in a sense, stealing the just efforts and creativity, hard work and sacrifices a person has put forth to earn or gain that property as their own.

Theft embraces a number of offenses, all of which take and keep another's property against the reasonable will of the owner. Examples include:

- ❏ the deliberate retention of borrowed or lost objects

Slavery

The seventh commandment condemns the hateful crime of enslaving others for profit, treating them as property to buy, sell, or exchange. No government or individual can justify this heinous crime for any reason—ever.

Gambling

Gambling does not violate justice if we do it honestly and reasonably and it does not bring harm upon ourselves or others. However, gambling is wrong when it deprives the gambler and

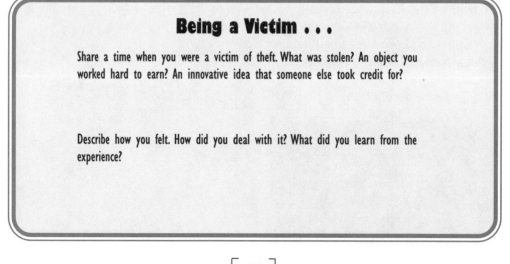

Being a Victim . . .

Share a time when you were a victim of theft. What was stolen? An object you worked hard to earn? An innovative idea that someone else took credit for?

Describe how you felt. How did you deal with it? What did you learn from the experience?

others whom the person gambling has responsibilities toward of the necessities of life. For example, it is wrong for a parent to gamble to the point that it renders him or her unable to support the family.

Stewardship

The creation story in the Book of Genesis teaches that God the Creator has given us dominion over the created universe. The word *dominion* comes from a word meaning "household." We have been given the responsibility to care for the household of God and to act as respectful stewards of God's gift of creation.

As responsible stewards, or caretakers, we are to take special care of the earth and the nonliving and living beings whose home it is. Pope John Paul II writes that we are to be "ministers charged with working in the name of God, who remains the sole owner in the full sense, since it is God's will that created goods should serve everyone in a just way" (*On the Coming of the Third Millennium*, 13).

Environment. We care responsibly for creation when we take care of the quality of life for all peoples of the earth—our neighbors. We consider not only the present needs of people but also the welfare of future generations. For example, we all know how burning fuel pollutes the air we breathe and the water we drink. Such practices contribute to the poor health not only of people living today but of those who will come after us for many generations. Working at discovering nonpolluting alternatives to meet our energy needs is one way we fulfill this responsibility.

Do Animals Have Rights?

Think about these issues and then respond using principles of Catholic morality.

Do animals have rights? Explain your position.

Is there a difference between experimenting on animals to test cosmetics and experimenting on animals to develop medicines or medical procedures that will save human lives? Explain your position.

Animals. Our dominion over the earth includes the proper **stewardship** of the animals who share the earth with us. What is our "relationship" to the animal population of the earth? The Catholic Church teaches that it is morally acceptable for us to use animals for the food and clothing necessary for our life. Similarly, rational medical experimentation on animals to save human life is also morally acceptable. However, to use animals for "extravagant wants" is wrong. Likewise, if we cause needless suffering and death of animals or spend extravagant sums of money on them to the neglect of people in our midst who are living in poverty, we are not acting as responsible stewards of the "household" of God.

Social Doctrine of the Catholic Church

As Christians we know that every person is endowed with the dignity of being created in the image of God and of being called to a life of love and friendship with God.

Since the nineteenth century, the **social justice teaching** of the Church has developed in response to the problems of industrialization. This social teaching, guided by the Holy Spirit, interprets historical events in light of the Gospel of Jesus Christ. It involves three elements:

❏ principles for reflection,

❏ criteria for judgment,

❏ guidelines for action.

These elements apply the gospel message to the systems, structures, and institutions of society, because all human relationships take place within them.

Peace and Justice

Led by the Spirit of God, the Catholic Church guides and teaches us how to live with this dignity and seek our vocation to a life of love and friendship with God. The Church calls everyone to base their lives on justice and peace— two virtues that support human dignity and are at the foundation of the kingdom of God.

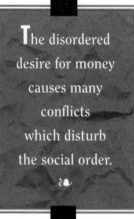

The disordered desire for money causes many conflicts which disturb the social order.

The Church exercises this responsibility by applying the Gospel to the political, economic, and social orders. It especially does this whenever the fundamental rights of the person or the salvation of souls requires it. Justice and peace not only deal with the common good of society but also affect our relationship with God, who is our ultimate goal. In fidelity to Jesus, the Church calls everyone—both individuals and the societies in which we live—to make these virtues part of the fabric of their lives.

The Gospel. The basis of the social teachings of the Catholic Church is respect for the individual as another self. Jesus taught respect and love of everyone, even our enemies. In a special way, we are to respond to people living in poverty and to those who are disadvantaged in other ways. When we work for social justice, we are putting our faith into action. We are taking the gospel message of peace and justice into the war against poverty, violence, and injustice, because these threaten or destroy the dignity and rights of people.

Guidance of the Holy Spirit. The Holy Spirit is our inspiration and strength to promote the Gospel on earth. Jesus is our model and guide. We look to them to lead us in building our world on the justice and peace proclaimed in the Scriptures—and not on any philosophical or political system that might be in fashion.

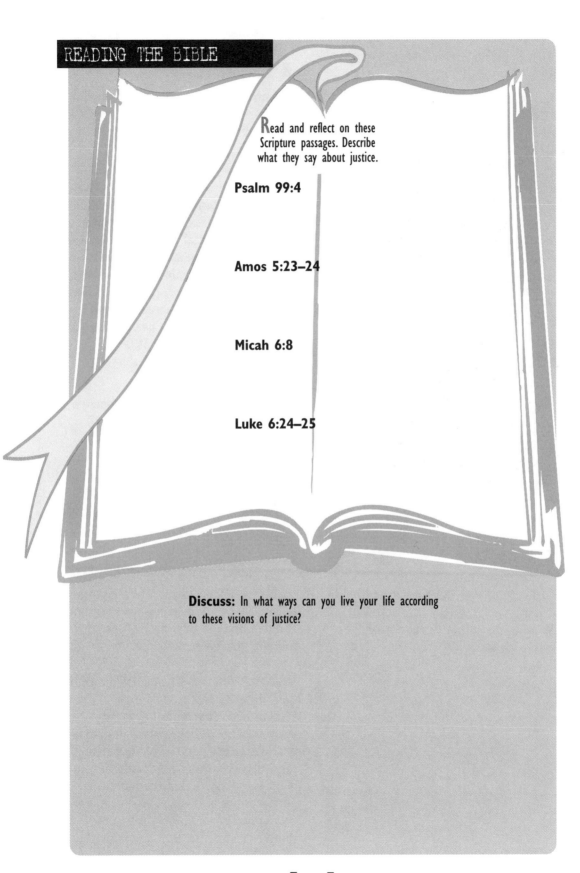

Read and reflect on these Scripture passages. Describe what they say about justice.

Psalm 99:4

Amos 5:23–24

Micah 6:8

Luke 6:24–25

Discuss: In what ways can you live your life according to these visions of justice?

Justice

The seventh commandment requires that our relationships with others are just. The Catholic Tradition distinguishes the following types of justice:

- **Commutative justice** regulates relations between individuals. It requires the restitution of stolen goods.

- **Legal justice** deals with our duties as citizens and what we owe the community.

- **Distributive justice** governs what the community owes citizens according to their contributions and needs.

How are each of these forms of justice lived out each day? List your examples.

If a person finds himself or herself in a life-or-death situation and takes food from a store, is that person stealing? Explain your views.

The Foundation of the Social Order

We can review Catholic social doctrine by focusing on the areas of economics, solidarity among nations, and love for people who are poor.

Economic and Political Systems. We create the systems and structures that form the foundation of the economic, political, and social orders in which we live. We base these systems and structures on values people judge to serve the common good. We must remember that the center of all economic and social life is the human person and the common good of people. It is not profit, power, or the possession of material goods.

As the Church, we have always spoken out against any social, political, or economic system that is contrary to the dignity of the human person. Therefore, the Church has always warned against any system that makes profit the *only* norm and ultimate goal of economic activity. Systems that make humans a mere means to profit include totalitarian, atheistic, and communistic economic theories and governments, and also unbridled capitalism. All these make money their god and dehumanize persons. All are morally unacceptable.

Economic Justice. The central point of Catholic teaching concerning economics is that we believe that everyone should have access in justice and love to the goods that God created for everyone's benefit. As Catholics we believe and assert that the human person is not at the service of the economy. The economy must serve individuals and the human community.

Work

With these fundamental principles in mind, the Church teaches:

❏ **Work is both a right and a duty.** Work is a right because God calls us to co-create with him by subduing the earth.

❏ Through work we are able to provide for ourselves and our families and serve one another.

❏ Through work we honor and bless God. Our work becomes a means to develop and use our God-given talents.

❏ Work is also a way for us to grow in holiness. By addressing the difficulties of work, we can participate in Christ's work of redemption. By being aware of the presence of Christ in our lives, we bring him and his values to our jobs. By being honest, loving, and moral Christian workers, we attract others to our Lord.

❏ Work can lead to conflicts between different interests. For example, labor unions, businesspersons, and public authorities may not always see eye-to-eye on issues. We are to strive to settle conflicts peacefully, through negotiation and arbitration whenever possible, when they arise.

❏ As workers we have the right to strike, to attain a just and proportionate benefit when arbitration and other peaceful means fail. We may not resort to violence in strikes nor use strikes as weapons to damage the common good. In making our decision to strike, we are to consider the negative impact it will have on innocent persons—those not directly involved in our disputes.

What Do You Think?

What is your view of working?

Is a job a gift or a burden?

Describe a person you admire because of their approach to work.

❏ Workers have the right to government support and protection. Government authorities must guarantee individual freedom to pursue the opportunity to seek employment. They are to work at maintaining a stable currency, protecting private property, and assuring the security that enables workers to benefit from their efforts.

- All qualified workers are to have the opportunity for employment without discrimination of gender, race, disability, religion, and so on. Unemployment insults a person's dignity, upsets stable living, and affects family in a negative way.

- Everyone has the right to a just wage. Profit alone should not determine a "just" wage. The economic demands of living in a society should also be considered in arriving at a "just" wage that is also a living wage. Considering what workers need to support themselves and their dependents is necessary to create a just and peaceful society.

- Workers must give an honest day's work for an honest day's pay. If the law requires it, they must pay social security taxes.

- Employers must prudently consider the economic and ecological impact of their businesses. They must always judge their decisions by their impact on people. Economic policy makers should always ask: What does the economy do *for* and *to* people? They must especially weigh the impact of their decisions and policies on those who are living in poverty and with other special needs.

Global Solidarity

We live in a society that is among the most economically developed nations in the world. But we live side by side with nations in which the majority of people are living in abject poverty and suffer death from famine and disease on a daily basis. The true development of nations and peoples should concern itself with the "development" of the whole person. It needs to concern itself not only with the "material" needs of peoples—but also the spiritual. True development fosters our vocation, or calling, to respond to God's call to share in his very life and love.

Many factors—for example, social, economic, and political policies that prevent development—cause inequitable debts that strangle a nation's economy. They foster unequal trade relations among nations, and promote the arms race, all of which help keep people living in conditions that attack their dignity and are serious obstacles to their living their vocation.

Poorer nations belong to the household of God. People living in poverty, suffering from famine and disease, are part of the household of God. In justice and charity, developed and wealthier nations must recognize their solidarity with and responsibility toward these poorer nations. When they meet these responsibilities, they are acting as true stewards of creation. They can do so through:

- direct aid to nations suffering the tragic results of natural catastrophes, famines, epidemics, and so on.

- reform of international economic and financial institutions to help promote more equality and equity in the relations between wealthier and poorer nations.

- support of the efforts of developing countries that are trying to work for growth and human freedom.

- support of Third World agricultural movements, because so many of the people living in poverty in the world are working on farms.

Love for others, and in the first place love for the poor, in whom the Church sees Christ himself, is made concrete in the promotion of justice. Justice will never be fully attained unless people see in the poor person, who is asking for help in order to survive, not an annoyance or a burden, but an opportunity for showing kindness and a chance for greater enrichment.

On the Hundredth Anniversary, 58

In what way can individuals, local communities, and nations work to "fully attain" justice?

Special Love for the Poor

We bear the name *Christian*. What does that mean? Jesus insists it included a practical, day-to-day love for the poor.

From the very first days of the Church, we have reached out to the poor as Jesus did and as Jesus taught us to do. He said, "Give to the one who asks of you, and do not turn your back on one who wants to borrow" (Matthew 5:42). In stronger terms, he warned us that he would judge us on what we do to the "least" living among us (see Matthew 25:40, 45).

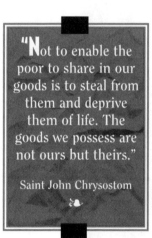

"**N**ot to enable the poor to share in our goods is to steal from them and deprive them of life. The goods we possess are not ours but theirs."

Saint John Chrysostom

As Christians we have a "preferential" love for people who are "poor." We show preferential love for the poor by putting the works of mercy into action. We work for the relief, the defense, and the freedom of the poor and those who have other needs through works of charity and mercy.

We value **almsgiving** as an important work of justice and love. Almsgiving involves sharing our time, talent, and possessions—money, clothes, and other essentials necessary for life—with people in need.

A God-centered life will help us realize that the purpose of material goods includes the use of them to help human beings on their journey to God. Rediscovering God will also help individuals and nations stop exploiting people who live in poverty or have other special needs. Living as people or countries that are "poor in spirit" will help us be aware of God's activity—Father, Son, and Holy Spirit—in our midst. It calls us to be loving persons who care for one another—especially the weak and poor.

The key responsibility for translating Christ's message of peace and justice into concrete deeds belongs to laypeople, not the clergy. According to our vocation and talents, we must actively promote social justice in the marketplace. We must proclaim Christ Jesus to a world that greatly needs him—and seek to build and live in the kingdom he announced.

How do I show compassion to others?

Compassion enables us to identify with the suffering of others and then to respond in a positive way to help others deal with that suffering. Mother Teresa of Calcutta, who died in 1997, taught us that working with the poor is to do "something beautiful for God." We do so when we show our compassion for people. Traditionally, Catholics have shown Christ-like compassion when they practice the corporal and spiritual works of mercy. These are:

Corporal Works of Mercy

1. Feed the hungry.
2. Give drink to the thirsty.
3. Clothe the naked.
4. Visit the imprisoned.
5. Shelter the homeless.
6. Visit the sick.
7. Bury the dead.

Spiritual Works of Mercy

1. Counsel the doubtful.
2. Instruct the ignorant.
3. Admonish sinners.
4. Comfort the afflicted.
5. Forgive offenses.
6. Bear wrongs patiently.
7. Pray for the living and the dead.

Discuss: List realistic examples of things you could do to put each of the works of mercy into practice.

IMPORTANT TERMS TO KNOW

almsgiving—sharing our possessions such as money, clothes, and other essentials for living with people in need

avarice—the inordinate passion for wealth and the power that comes with it

covetousness—the inordinate and unjust desire for possessing what rightfully belongs to another person

envy—the inordinate desire for the possessions that belong to someone else

greed—the unchecked desire to amass earthly goods

justice—the cardinal virtue that renders to each person what is his or her due by right

social justice teaching—the Church's body of doctrine that applies the gospel message of Jesus to society, its institutions, and its political and economic structures

stewardship—the God-given responsibility of all people to respect creation and to use it to enhance the dignity of all and to enable people to live their vocation as a person created in the image and likeness of God

Works of Mercy—fourteen ways named by the Church that help us live Christ's command to love others by helping them care for their bodily and spiritual needs

CHAPTER SUMMARY

The Spirit calls and guides us to live justly. In this chapter we learned:

1. The seventh commandment requires us to live justly. It commands justice and charity in the stewardship of earthly goods and the results of human work.

2. Everyone has a right to private property. But the ownership and use of goods is meant for the common good and not merely for the benefit of the owner.

3. The seventh commandment forbids theft, which includes such acts as fraud, paying unjust wages, inferior work, tax evasion, corrupt business practices, waste, forgery, and destruction of private and public property. Taking and using another person's property unjustly requires restitution.

4. The dominion over creation demands that we care for the environment, preserving it for both current and future generations.

5. Whenever human rights or the salvation of souls requires it, the Church's social justice teaching applies gospel truths to the political, economic, and social orders.

6. The author, center, and goal of economic and social life is the human person, and not profit, power, or material goods.

7. Work is a right and a duty. By means of work, we take part in the work of creation and redemption.

8. The tenth commandment teaches us to avoid coveting unjustly what belongs to another. It forbids avarice and envy, which are capital sins.

9. Economic justice, global solidarity, and a preferential option for people who are poor are foundations of Catholic social doctrine. Almsgiving and the spiritual and corporal works of mercy are concrete ways Christians can put their faith into action.

EXPLORING OUR CATHOLIC FAITH

1. Listening to God's Word

Read and reflect on James 2:15–17. In what ways is the Spirit helping us understand what it means to live justly and compassionately?

2. Understanding the Teachings of the Catholic Church

The *Catechism of the Catholic Church* teaches that the human person is the "author, center, and goal of all economic and social life" (2459). What does this mean? What are some of the signs that this teaching is not being lived out?

3. Reflecting on Our Catholic Faith

Saint John Chrysostom wrote: "Not to enable the poor to share in our goods is to steal from them and deprive them of life. The goods we possess are not ours but theirs." In what ways are you living this insight into our faith? In what ways do you resist living it? Write your thoughts in your journal.

4. Living Our Catholic Faith

What opportunities exist in your community for you to live justly? In what ways can you work with others to live justly? In what ways can your parish community help you?

CHAPTER 10

The Eighth Commandment: Speak and Live the Truth

The Spirit is the one that testifies,
and the Spirit is truth.

1 JOHN 5:6

What Do You Think?

Match the terms in the right column with the descriptions in the left column.

_____ 1. assuming as true, without enough evidence, the moral fault of another

_____ 2. without a valid reason, revealing another person's faults

_____ 3. lying that harms the reputation of another

_____ 4. speaking a falsehood with the intention to deceive

_____ 5. lying under oath

A.   Lie

B.   Calumny

C.   Detraction

D.   Perjury

E.   Rash Judgment

An often told, true story concerns an 11-year-old contestant from South Carolina who made it to the fourth round of a national spelling contest in Washington. The contestant was to spell the word *avowal.* When the contestant did so, the judges were not able to agree on whether an *"a"* or *"e"* was used for the second-to-the-last letter. The Southern accent confused them. Even after listening to a tape playback, they could not decipher what was said. Finally, the chief judge asked, "How did you spell the word?"

By this time, the contestant knew what the correct spelling was because so many in the auditorium had been whispering it. Nevertheless, the contestant told the judges, "I misspelled the word," and graciously left the stage.

When have you so honestly admitted error when confronted? What were the consequences? Do you find being "so" honest difficult? Explain.

At the contestant's courageous show of honesty, the entire audience, including fifty reporters, leapt to their feet and gave her an ovation. A follower of Jesus is honorable: honest, truthful, and dependable. The eighth commandment teaches us how to be truthful people. This chapter will study the eighth commandment and conclude with a personal review of the Ten Commandments.

(Catechism of the Catholic Church, 2464–2474)

Truth

The eighth commandment guides us in living as truthful people. "Truth or truthfulness is the virtue which consists in showing oneself true in deeds and truthful in words, and guarding against duplicity, dissimulation, and hypocrisy" (CCC, 2505).

When we are truthful, we bear witness to God, who is the source of all truth. The virtue of truthfulness, candor or sincerity, is related to the cardinal virtue of justice. When we are truthful, we are being just, because each person is due the truth. Without this virtue, we could not live together in trust.

> "**H**onor is better than honors."
>
> Abraham Lincoln

God Is Truth

The Old Testament reveals God is truth, and the source of all truth. Both his word and his law are truth. He wants his people to live in the truth. Because we are made in the image and likeness of God, we are called to be people of truth.

God wills his children to be like him, to be people of truth. God implanted in our nature an inclination toward truth. It is part of our human dignity to embrace the truth once we know it and live our lives according to what truth requires.

Jesus, "The Truth"

Jesus Christ, God-made-flesh, revealed himself to be "the way and the truth and the life" (John 14:6). He calls us, his followers, to be people of the truth. He instructs, "Let your 'Yes' mean 'Yes,' and your 'No' mean 'No.' Anything more is from the evil one" (Matthew 5:37).

Jesus has also sent us the Spirit of Truth to lead us to the truth. (See John 14:26; 16:13.) We are to witness to the truth in our ordinary, day-to-day affairs by living the truth of the Gospel. We are to proclaim him to others in word and deed. Knowing and living the truth Jesus revealed will set us free. (See John 8:31–32.)

Martyrs are those who gave up their lives to witness to Jesus and the Gospel. Their courage to lay down their lives inspires us to be truthful in daily life. Their sacrifice for the Lord inspires us to share our Christian faith with others.

The Bible teaches us, in many passages, the value and importance of being truthful. Read and reflect on these Scripture verses. In your own words, tell what these Scripture verses tell you about "truth."

Sirach 4:28

Even to the death fight for truth, and the LORD your God will battle for you.

John 3:21

But whoever lives the truth comes to the light, so that his works may be clearly seen as done by God.

John 8:31–32

Jesus then said to those Jews who believed in him, "If you remain in my word, you will truly be my disciples, and you will know the truth, and the truth will set you free."

John 18:37–38

So Pilate said to him, "Then you are a king?" Jesus answered, "You say I am a king. For this I was born and for this I came into the world, to testify to the truth. Everyone who belongs to the truth listens to my voice." Pilate said to him, "What is truth?"

Dishonoring the Truth

The eighth commandment instructs us not to bear false witness, that is, not to misrepresent the truth when relating to others. It calls us to be a person of integrity, one who is without malice, guile, insincerity, and the like. As followers of Jesus we are called to speak the truth honestly—people whose word can be trusted.

These acts are contrary to living the eighth commandment.

Lying. **Lying** is the most common abuse against truth and is always wrong. Jesus condemned it as the devil's work. A lie is speaking a falsehood to deceive another. Lying is an injustice. Its purpose is to lead into error someone who has a right to know the truth. Its deception keeps others who have the right to know the truth from knowing the truth.

The seriousness of lying depends on several factors: the circumstances, the intentions of the liar, the harm it causes, and the nature of the truth the lie deforms. For example, lying to your teacher about why you did not do your homework last night would usually be considered a venial sin. However, speaking outright falsehoods to destroy another person's reputation would be mortally sinful.

You have probably heard the expression "little white lies." In reality, there is no such thing as a "white" lie. A very real danger is that shading the truth can become habitual. We think nothing of lying; it becomes our second nature.

Whenever we sin against justice and truth we have a grave duty to repent, seek forgiveness, and try to repair any damage we have caused. We must admit to the lie and then tell the truth. As best as humanly possible, we must try to undo any harm we may have caused another's reputation, for example, by contacting all those who may have heard our lies. To do anything less than this is not worthy of a Christian.

Harmonious human relationships begin in truth. When a lie enters the scene, discord takes root. Society suffers the consequences because trust is lacking. The door is open to all kinds of evils against the truth, such as broken promises, character assassination, revenge, and the like.

Hypocrisy. A common form of lying is hypocrisy. Hypocrites pretend to have certain beliefs or feelings or virtues that they do not, in truth, possess. Derived from the Greek word *hypokrisis* for "play acting," hypocrites put on masks, hoping others will think well of them. A common example of a hypocrite is someone who puts on a smiling face and speaks nice words to your face while thinking the opposite or talking behind your back.

Bragging. Bragging is boasting about accomplishments and the like that have no basis in reality. Bragging distorts the truth and deceives others.

False Witness and Perjury. A lie told in court is false witness. Lying under oath is perjury. Callous disregard for the truth in court undermines a justice system that tries to seek the truth. **Perjury** destroys fairness. The harm caused by these kinds of lies is great. Innocent people might be punished; guilty people let off; punishment unnecessarily increased.

Rash judgment. Everyone has the right to a good reputation. We should do everything in our power to preserve a person's honor because once it is lost, getting it back again is very difficult. When we judge someone rashly, we assume the truth of some moral fault in the person accused without sufficient basis. When

we listen and encourage gossip we are often guilty of **rash judgment.**

We can work to avoid rashly judging others by putting the best possible interpretation on other people's thoughts, words, and actions. If we are unsure about something, we should ask

Can I Keep a Secret?

We should never lie. Does this mean that everyone has an absolute right to the truth in every situation? In a concrete situation, Christian charity and prudence will sometimes tell us that we should not reveal everything we know. When the safety and good of others or someone's privacy rights or the common good are at stake, sometimes silence or discreet language might be the best policy.

We should underscore the important Catholic teaching about the "sacramental seal of confession." For no reason ever may a confessor reveal by word or any other way what has been revealed to him by a penitent. This seal of confession is so sacred that if a priest should violate it he would be automatically excommunicated.

In a similar vein, professional secrets, for example, those learned by doctors and lawyers, must be kept confidential. The only exception would be those very rare cases where keeping the secret would cause grave harm to the confider, confidante, or a third party. An example here might be a friend who told you in secrecy that he is thinking about committing suicide. If this should ever happen, out of love for your friend, please immediately seek the help of an adult or call the suicide hot line for advice on how to proceed.

for clarification rather than first simply condemn others and make a negative judgment about them. If that is not possible, we should always give others the benefit of the doubt.

Detraction and Calumny. Honoring the truth requires us to respect other people, their reputations, and their right to privacy. When we reveal, without a good reason, someone's faults and failings to others who were unaware of them, we commit **detraction.** When we tell lies about others that damage their reputations and that cause others to judge them negatively, we commit **calumny.** Detraction and calumny are offenses against both justice and charity. Everyone has a right to a good reputation, respect, and honor. These two sins are evils that destroy others in one of the cruelest ways imaginable.

Irony. Irony is using words to convey the opposite of their literal meaning. Using irony to tear down a person or make fun of some aspect of their reputation is also wrong. Irony is often sarcastic because it cuts into a person to hurt him or her. It might make us laugh, but its purpose is to cut down, not build up.

Gossip. Gossip is the spreading of rumors about others. It often arises out of feelings of pride and superiority that result in a false sense of power over others. Gossip is often vicious. It is always cowardly and un-Christian. Because it does so much damage, growing more absurd with each retelling, we should avoid listening to and spreading gossip.

Flattery, Adulation, Complaisance.
Flattery and adulation consist of giving excessive or false praise to get on the good side of someone. Complaisance is "going along to get along." It cheerfully tries to please others. Not even friendship can justify this type of untrue speech that gives others the impression that they are doing just fine. When we commit acts of flattery, adulation, or complaisance to support another person's vices or grave sins, we become an accomplice in their sins.

You Decide

Please answer Yes (*Y*), No (*N*), or Unsure (*U*) to the following cases.

_____ 1. Would you do anything dishonest at work, especially if you would lose your job if you did not go along?

_____ 2. Would you tell a close friend that she has an annoying habit?

_____ 3. You discover that a good friend is rifling lockers during gym class. Would you turn him in?

_____ 4. A friend asks you to lie to her parents for her. Would you?

_____ 5. Do you say things that you don't mean out of politeness?

_____ 6. When writing a resume of extracurricular activities for a college application, would you exaggerate the number of activities?

_____ 7. If you were an employer, would you hire someone like you?

Discuss: Which of the activities above clearly violate the demands of the eighth commandment? Explain.

Explain your answer to question 7.

(CCC, 2493–2503)

Society and the Truth

As members of society we have a right to truthful, factual information. We also have the right to express ourselves freely. These rights are key social issues of our times.

Truth and the Media

The media affect our lives in unimaginable ways—from printed resources like newspapers and popular magazines to television and the movies to the Internet. The media are a dominating force in our culture today. They are a power for much good. At the same time, all these information outlets are proving themselves to be a source of great evil.

As members of society, we have a right to solid information from the media. But that information is to be rooted in truth, freedom, justice, and solidarity. Journalists must be fair and accurate in their reporting. Those who control the media have a profound duty to form and spread public opinion and the news in a just and charitable way.

While we have a right to information, every person also has a right to privacy. The media are to be very careful about exposing the personal lives of people in politics or other public figures. Often the common good is not advanced by all the revelations of the private lives of the "rich and famous."

We have a right to expect our public officials to safeguard the free and nonoffensive flow of information. Governments should resist any temptation to manipulate the media, for example, by politically controlling public opinion through twisting truth or a totalitarian agenda.

As users of the media, we are to exercise moderation and self-control. Likewise, we should not be passive observers who uncritically soak up what we observe. We should take an active role in using our minds and our Christian values to evaluate the information and entertainment to which we are exposed. We should take an active role to be watchful consumers of what is said or shown.

Truth, Beauty, and Art

We have been created in the image of God—who is Truth, who is Beauty. When we hear or read or experience the truth, it evokes a positive response in us. We sense its "beauty," its "rightness" in our hearts, its "harmony" with God's plan, its "connection" with God. Beauty signifies the true nature of our relationship with God and with God's creation.

Through art we can express the truth we discover about our relationship with God and about God's creation. Art can reveal the truth and beauty of God's presence in our world and in our lives. It can draw us to adore God, to pray to and love him.

Portraying the Truth

. . . .

List your top three favorite videos, songs, or television shows.

Evaluate how well each "tells" the truth.

1.

2.

3.

Share and discuss your responses with the members of your group.

Living the Ten Commandments

Without studying the following too carefully, what is the first thing you can decipher with these letters?

GODISNOWHERE

How did you answer? Many people who see this at first glance translate it to read:

GOD IS NOWHERE

Perhaps you are one of many who see it this way. If so, take another look. Note that this string of letters can also contain the message:

GOD IS NOW HERE.

Many people in today's world live as though God is not here. They ramble through life without a compass, blown by every fad and whimsy that come down the pike. They have no idea where they are going, and when they get there, they don't know how they did. Nor do they know where they have been.

It is not this way when we live a moral life. The point of view of the *Catechism of the Catholic Church* is that God is now here. We give witness to that truth when we live a moral life by living the commandments and the Gospel and the teachings of the Church.

Living a moral Christian life will bring us happiness in this life now and eternal happiness in the next. Living the Ten Commandments is the key to friendship with the Lord Jesus. Remember his teaching: "If you keep my commandments, you will remain in my love, just as I have kept my Father's commandments and remain in his love" (John 15:10).

May all of us grow in friendship with the Lord and live a happy life—despite the rough times! May we all meet again in eternity! God bless you on your journey.

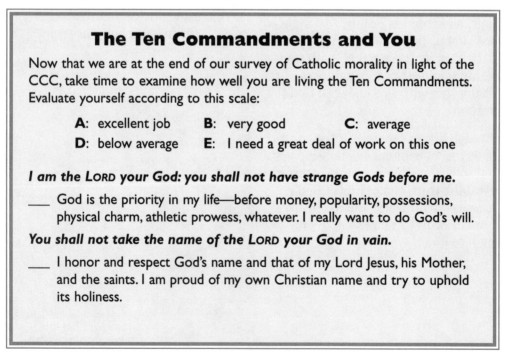

The Ten Commandments and You

Now that we are at the end of our survey of Catholic morality in light of the CCC, take time to examine how well you are living the Ten Commandments. Evaluate yourself according to this scale:

A: excellent job   **B**: very good   **C**: average
D: below average   **E**: I need a great deal of work on this one

I am the LORD your God: you shall not have strange Gods before me.

____ God is the priority in my life—before money, popularity, possessions, physical charm, athletic prowess, whatever. I really want to do God's will.

You shall not take the name of the LORD your God in vain.

____ I honor and respect God's name and that of my Lord Jesus, his Mother, and the saints. I am proud of my own Christian name and try to uphold its holiness.

Remember to keep holy the LORD's Day.

____ I celebrate the Eucharist each week. I set aside time to pray—to talk and listen to the Lord.

Honor your father and your mother.

____ I respect and obey my parents. I express gratitude to them. I obey proper authority figures. I am a cooperative family member and a good sibling.

You shall not kill.

____ I respect my life as a great gift. I am moderate in my habits. I respect other people and care especially for the poor and hurting. I avoid harmful practices.

You shall not commit adultery.

____ I am trying to live a sexually upright life by exercising the virtue of chastity. I respect my sexuality. I look on others as persons worthy of respect, not objects for self-gratification.

You shall not steal.

____ I respect the property of others. I do not take what does not belong to me. I treat others with justice, giving them their due.

You shall not bear false witness against your neighbor.

____ I am a person of truth. I neither lie nor cheat. I refuse to gossip. I respect and defend the good reputation of others.

You shall not covet your neighbor's wife.

____ I try to control my sexual urges by exercising the virtues of purity and modesty. I refuse to look at pornography.

You shall not covet your neighbor's goods.

____ I am grateful for my own gifts and the possessions God has allowed me to own. I am not envious of others, nor am I greedy.

Resolution:

I am going to try to improve in the area of

In the next two weeks, I resolve to do the following:

Prayer

Every person is called to be a person of honor and truth. As Christians we believe we have been given the Spirit of truth, who will lead us to know and to live the truth. We believe that to live as a person of honor and of truth, we need to be a person of prayer.

God be in my head

    and in my understanding.

God be in mine eyes

    and in my looking.

God be in my mouth

    and in my speaking.

God be in my heart

    and in my thinking.

God be at my end

    and my departing.

Sarum Primer, 1527

IMPORTANT TERMS TO KNOW

calumny—false statements made about others that harm their reputation and cause false judgments about them; slander

detraction—without a valid reason, revealing a person's faults to someone who did not know about them previously

lying—speaking a falsehood to deceive another who has a right to the truth

perjury—giving false witness under oath, as in a court of law

rash judgment—without sufficient evidence, assuming the moral fault of someone

CHAPTER SUMMARY

We have been created in the image and likeness of God, who is Truth. The eighth commandment calls us to be truthful in our words and deeds.

1. The virtue of truthfulness is a form of justice. It provides people with the truth that is necessary for harmonious living. Christians are to witness to the Gospel and Jesus Christ, who is the Truth-made-flesh. We look to the martyrs for inspiration to be persons of integrity.

2. The eighth commandment forbids lying, that is, speaking a falsehood to deceive another who has a right to the truth. A common form of lying is hypocrisy. Hypocrites pretend to be what they are not.

3. The eighth commandment also forbids false witness, perjury, rash judgment, detraction and calumny, flattery and complaisance.

4. We have a serious duty to repair any harm we cause whenever we sin against the virtues of justice or truth.

5. We are not obligated to reveal the truth to persons who do not have a right to it. For example, priests must never reveal what they learned in the confessional.

6. The media have the responsibility to present information truthfully and fairly. The use of the media should always be rooted in freedom, truth, justice, and solidarity.

7. Art can reveal the truth and beauty of God's presence in our world and in our lives. It can draw us to adore God, to pray to him and to love him.

EXPLORING OUR CATHOLIC FAITH

1. Listening to God's Word

John teaches, "If we say, 'We have fellowship with [Jesus Christ],' while we continue to walk in darkness, we lie and do not act in truth" (1 John 1:6). What do you think John is saying?

2. Understanding the Teachings of the Catholic Church

The bishops at the Second Vatican Council in their decree on the *Means of Social Communication* taught that the proper exercise of the right to provide information for the common good "demands that the content of the communication be true and—within the limits set by justice and charity—complete" (5). What demands does this teaching place upon journalists and others reporting the news?

3. Reflecting on Our Catholic Faith

Saint Ignatius Loyola wrote: "[E]very good Christian ought to be more eager to put a good interpretation on a neighbor's statement [rather] than to condemn it" (*Spiritual Exercises,* 22). In what ways does this insight into living our faith help you? Write your thoughts in your journal.

4. Living Our Catholic Faith

Brainstorm ways telling the truth helps oneself and helps others. Choose to use one of the responses to motivate yourself to speak the truth in a difficult situation this week.

Index